New Garden Design

New Garden Design

Inspiring Private Paradises

Zahid Sardar | Photographs by Marion Brenner

Gibbs Smith, Publisher

TO ENRICH AND INSPIRE HUMANKIND

Salt Lake City | Charleston | Santa Fe | Santa Barbara

First Edition
12 11 10 09 08   5 4 3 2 1

Text © 2008 Zahid Sardar
Photographs © 2008 Marion Brenner

Published by
Gibbs Smith, Publisher
P.O. Box 667
Layton, Utah 84041

Orders: 1.800.835.4993
www.gibbs-smith.com

Designed by Zahid Sardar
Printed and bound in Hong Kong

Library of Congress Cataloging-in-
Publication Data

Sardar, Zahid.
New garden design : inspiring private
paradises / Zahid Sardar ;
photographs by Marion
Brenner. — 1st ed.
p. cm.
Includes bibliographical
references.
ISBN-13: 978-1-4236-0334-4
ISBN-10: 1-4236-0334-6
1. Gardens—Design. 2.
Gardens—California—
Design. I. Title.
SB472.45.S227 2008
712'.6—dc22

2008005674

PAGE 2: The 1950s Donnell Garden in Sonoma. PAGE 4: The Anderson Cactus Garden near San Diego. FRONTISPIECE: The Kramlich Garden in Napa.

ACKNOWLEDGMENTS

With heartfelt thanks to friends, designers and home owners who have graciously shared their work and to our friends: Alta Tingle of the Gardener, Flora Grubb and Jason Dewees of Flora Grubb Gardens, Antonia Adezio and Betsy Flack of The Garden Conservancy, and the Strybing Arboretum in San Francisco. Special thanks to Kelly Macy for her generous advice.

For our families

Contents

INTRODUCTION
THE FIRST GARDENS

Garden design has evolved from rudimentary farming into an art form, thanks to serendipitous juxtapositions of cultures, grafted one upon the other. While no one can tell conclusively where the first cultivated garden was, more than likely it was in the arid Middle East where most of the world's oldest civilizations began, and today, new garden designs still reflect their seminal form.

To imagine that form, flash back 4,000 years to the oases gardens of desert nomads and to towns that preceded Judeo/Christian and Islamic societies. There, discover the roots of Paradise—the ancient Persian *pairidaeza* (walled garden) and a rectangular walled park, or *firdaus,* where nobles hunted amid springs, orchards and gardens stocked with wildlife, protected from storms and marauders—and glimpse the genesis of ancient Greek, Roman and modern American gardens.

ABOVE: At her Berkeley home and gallery garden, artist Marcia Donahue incorporates found objects, gravestones and stone sculpture of her own making that echoes ancient works in the Easter Islands.

RIGHT: At the new de Young Museum in San Francisco, which was built over former sand dunes, landscape architect Walter Hood has created a biblical garden of tree ferns and shattered or crushed shale—to suggest how the sand on the site was probably created over time.

Taming nature—attractive, yet dangerous—is one way to be closer to it and gardeners from antiquity to today, in Greek *topias,* farms, or contemporary urban backyards, have been transfixed by the idea. It's a small wonder that gardens play a key role in stories of the oldest religions. In the desert, a paradise garden was akin to heaven.

The well-watered garden was a symbol of life, peace and prosperity. Hydraulic systems mastered by Mesopotamians, Persians and Assyrians to feed orchards and fountains on higher ground near river marshes, and ancient Egyptian rooftop gardens, distinctive peristyle colonnaded courtyards, and water gardens stocked with fish and fowl for the afterlife along the Nile, all influenced the Greeks.

No examples of paintings or frescoes of those pre-Hellenistic gardens in Greece have survived to tell us more, but their affinity for nature and descriptions of their sacred grottos and groves, kitchen gardens, courts and hunting grounds derived from Persian originals come to us through the stories of bards such as Homer.

In 332 BC when Alexander the Great ventured into Egypt from Macedonia, founding Alexandria, and then east to India, he was exposed along the way to elaborate Persian and Assyrian versions of enclosed outdoor space. Although he died far from home in 323 BC, his armies returned with new plants (such as *tulsi,* basil from India) and ideas for gardens with hydraulic irrigation that the Greeks emulated. *Paradeisos,* hunting parks and outdoor shrines with statues of deities under shelters (like tents in oases), evolved into open pavilions and covered temple buildings in gardens.

Walled Roman pleasure gardens with frescoes, such as those preserved at Pompeii, show how the Greeks before them must have tried to shape their sacred parks and gardens. Kitchen gardens, we learn from ancient chroniclers, were within paved open-to-sky courts outside a one-room house and may have had potted herbs and plants, while horticultural space for vegetables and flowers grown in the ground was usually within shouting distance of the town gate.

Vitruvius's writings circa 27 BC are the oldest surviving manual on design, and his adage about buildings that must have durability, utility and delight can be extended to enclosed outdoor space. When volcanic ash from Mount Vesuvius buried Pompeii and Herculaneum in AD 79, it also took the life of Pliny the Elder whose writings best depict Roman garden concepts. He died in the tragedy that has also miraculously

preserved one of antiquity's garden cities, but his words and Vitruvius's treatise bring to life what remains of Pompeii and other such Mediterranean garden sites.

Emperor Hadrian's AD 130 villa garden outside Rome showed eclectic ideas from areas of the world he had visited, including lavish use of water in the Egyptian style. It had grottos, canals and pools, enclosed domestic gardens and open courtly spaces, and theaters for public gatherings all arranged to take advantage of the location. Classical gardens typically relied on prescribed forms that made Hadrian's innovations a better model for many adventurous mannerist Italian, French

squares by two intersecting rills or channels of water running the length and breadth of the garden with a sacred pavilion in the center. Indigenous Indian versions of the quartered garden, planted as a *mandala* per Hindu *Vastu* tradition, were dedicated to fire, water, earth and ether, and, with each caravan along the Silk Route passing through India, these formal and metaphysical garden notions seeped into Europe during the Middle Ages.

Medieval cloisters and churches became laboratories for herbal remedies and healing gardens laid out in parterres where the mythic and medicinal properties of ivy, myrtle, olive, pomegranate and rosemary—ubiquitous in cultic Greek gardens dedicated to Aphrodite or Artemis—were better understood. Add to that the Moorish taste for tiled, inward-looking, water-filled gardens with few but fragrant plants in Spain under Ottoman rule, and you have a view of the first Euro/American West Coast gardens that came north from Spanish Mexico. Just 200 years ago Christian missionaries from San Diego to San Francisco were planting practical four-square paradise gardens in walled courtyards with stone fonts in the center.

With Japanese and Chinese immigrants in California came a garden philosophy descended from feng shui and Buddhist Zen ideas—raked sand to simulate water, reflecting pools to grab the sky, and curving walkways to shake off evil spirits. Eastern and Western garden ideas once again were able to mesh.

Architect Frank Lloyd Wright embraced the Japanese aesthetic and later-1930s-to-mid-century California designers such as Thomas Church, Garret Eckbo and Robert Royston influenced by the modern art of Joan Miro, Jean Arp, Paul Klee, Antoni Gaudi and architects such as Alvar Alto, laid the ground for artful free-form garden layouts and Zen-like abstraction.

Their goal was to bring the outdoors in and to open homes to the exterior—almost in opposition to the idea of a walled garden. Landscape architect Lawrence Halprin aimed for an even more naturalistic look, suggesting, at the seminal 1960s

and Mediterranean gardens built after the villa was rediscovered during the Renaissance. At the 1550 Villa d'Este in Tivoli, where cascading fountains are fed by the river Aniene, statuary was literally lifted from Hadrian's estate. Twentieth-century Hearst Castle in San Simeon by architect Julia Morgan owes a debt to Hadrian's design.

The classic *charbagh* (quartered garden) of Islamic palaces and tombs, which came to represent paradise or heaven, can be seen in its developed stage at the Taj Mahal, built by the Mughal emperors of India. Their fragrant gardens were the zenith of the ancient rectangular walled compound form divided into four

Sea Ranch development along the Marin Headlands, that buildings ought to be visually one with the land, and gardens ought not to feel enclosed. Halprin's updated Stern Grove, a nature preserve and natural amphitheater in San Francisco, has hand-hewn bleachers set in terraces to look like ancient foundations in a grassy archaeological site. These borderless garden ideas are the basis of many new gardens today.

Abstract, modern gardens, such as the ones these designers created, often have horizontal planes such as decks and bridges thrusting into the landscape where open spaces are abundant. Interior spaces open freely onto exterior decks—"outdoor rooms"—that surround pools. Massed plantings and groves of trees are arranged not so much for color but for texture and form.

Church's 1956 kidney-shaped pool for the Donnell family in Sonoma, an hour north of San Francisco, is synonymous with modernism and abstraction in America. It is not surprising that on the West Coast, where Eastern and Western ideas merge more fully, there is the greatest concentration of new garden designs that steer clear of Renaissance formality or pure Islamic geometry.

The movies and Hollywood had an impact on garden design through the work of set garden designers such as Florence Yoch whose refinements for the celluloid world were frequently emulated by gardeners in real life.

With each succeeding interpretation, the prototypal four-square gardens from 4,000 years ago evolved into free-form sacred or profane, public or private, decorative or merely practical gardens over time.

The American West Coast garden today, abstract in design and with seemingly no connection to the formalities of a paradise garden or its Persian, Indian or Greco-Roman and

Mediterranean antecedents, echoes them all. Walls, fountains, pavilions, canals, pools, terraces and groves appear in unexpected ways.

New Garden Design is not definitive, but the book covers a range of interpretations today. West Coast weather varies from desert conditions in Southern California to Mediterranean farther north, foggy in the San Francisco Bay Area, and year-round rain in Oregon and Washington, making the gardens in this book models for most of the country.

New Garden Design also aims to show how many ancient lessons haven't been forgotten.

For instance, Alcatraz Island—an enclosed space—in San Francisco Bay is swathed in the overgrown ruins of gardens planted by settlers in 1865, the wives of army officers when it was a garrison, and families of prison officials when it became a penitentiary. It is a kind of modern library of foreign plants—such as those in a Persian *firdaus* or medieval monastery—that survives despite the forty years of neglect that followed the island's closure as a federal prison. Since 2003 the efforts of The Garden Conservancy based in the San Francisco Presidio are helping to revive and maintain the historic gardens that are now completely naturalized.

Alcatraz predates many arboretums and university botanical gardens that have deliberately modeled themselves after medieval monastery gardens. Ironically, it was a barren rock surrounded by the bay and thrived only when it was cultivated like an oases garden with several rare plants.

Like Alexander's generals and the first horticulturists (from *hortus*, or garden in Latin and *khortos* in Greek), the Bay Area's

Hortisexualists, a club of about a dozen gardeners in San Jose, Berkeley, Lafayette and Oakland, continue to propagate and cross pollinate different species of plants. The group grew quite innocuously out of a need to visit gardens open only to professional organizations. Paradise's walls have become backdrops or seats; formal or symmetrical Italian Renaissance gardens are reinterpreted as modern parterres, sculpture gardens or fields of one kind of plant; temples and pavilions reappear as follies—Chinese pagodas, tree houses and even giant Druid mushrooms. In one San Francisco garden by artist Shirley Watts, a translucent plastic pavilion with no roof is a lens to view the sky, inspired perhaps by artist James Turrell's volcanic crater studio. In a lavender garden in Sonoma, giant *paraguas* (Spanish for umbrella) are modern hypostyle halls such as those lotus capital colonnades at Egyptian Queen Hatshepsut's lakeside temple at Deir el-Bahri, the oldest-surviving example of landscape architecture. A viticultural pond in northern California's wine country is transformed into a primordial lake paces away from a Tuscan-style *potager*.

Garden ideas spring from many sources, and for caravans of tourists, the Cornerstone Festival of Gardens in Sonoma, modeled after Chaumont-sur-Loire in France, is an encyclopedia of new garden types from West Coast designers such as Topher Delaney, Walter Hood, Ron Lutsko, Andrea Cochran, Andy Cao and Pamela Burton, many of whom have worked on gardens included in this book.

Cornerstone—launched in 2004 and the first such garden in the United States—is a modern sculpture park where the

FACING: Los Angeles landscape designer Pamela Burton created "Earth Walk," a temporary garden at the Cornerstone Festival of Gardens, an hour north of San Francisco. Burton's creation is a sloping ramp cut into the earth. It leads to what she considers the heart of any garden: rich soil. Down below, obscured from full view by tall grasses, a slender bench beside a pond with lotuses and fish is a place to sit and think.
TOP RIGHT: A dying Monterey pine swathed in sky-blue plastic balls by Claude Cormier has become Cornerstone's billboard and de facto logo. The festival itself is the brainchild of Chris Hougie, an entrepreneur inspired to found the first American showcase of contemporary garden design after a 1996 visit to the annual garden festival at Chaumont, France. In the foreground, purple and red plastic pinwheel daisies by Kenneth Smith spin and turn in the high-afternoon winds.
RIGHT: Cornerstone was laid out in a grid pattern by San Francisco landscape architect Ron Lutsko, who designed its Corten steel entry gate.

CLOCKWISE FROM LEFT: In San Francisco's Golden Gate Park, the new de Young Museum, designed by Pritzker award-winning Swiss architects Herzog and De Meuron, meshes with gardens by Walter Hood that surround it or thrust inside the building into glass vitrines—which are a new kind of glass-walled garden; a giant safety pin sculpture by Claes Oldenberg presides in the museum's sculpture garden, which is crisscrossed with crushed shale and asphalt brick paths; Hood's checkerboard planting pattern is broken by grassy mounds or stacked shale.
FACING, TOP RIGHT: The winning design by Jensen & Macy Architects and CMG Landscape Architecture for a new sculpture garden atop the San Francisco Museum of Modern Art shows galleries overlooking a walled garden. Jensen Architects will build the project.
FACING: For a garden in Hillsborough, south of San Francisco, designer Ron Lutsko created a private spa with corner walls high enough to sit on. It will eventually be surrounded by flowering magnolias, wild strawberries and veronica 'Georgia Blue' accent stone pavers.

gardens are frequently built and not grown. A dying tree covered in blue plastic balls is a fitting symbol for some of those gardens that have nothing growing.

Walter Hood's conceptual gardens—beds filled with shale shards and pebbles to represent the forming of sand dunes on which the site was formed—for the Herzog & De Meuron–designed de Young Museum, and artist Robert Irwin's painterly terraced garden for the Paul Getty Museum by architect Richard Meier in Los Angeles are the new form of public garden inspired by art as well as nature.

The new garden is a pleasure garden but vested with spiritual, symbolic and ecological intent. It is still a place to tame and view nature, built, as Vitruvius required, with *firmitas, utilitas* and *venustas*, "beauty" in Latin. Increasingly garden designers and artists are leading the way to eco-consciousness. To plant correctly, organic mulches and non-toxic soil amendments are not enough. A designer has to avoid invasive plants such as pampas grass, which has no natural predators on the West Coast, cautions Flora Grubb, founder of an experimental garden design studio and plant nursery in San Francisco. Museums are also leading the way. In San Francisco's Golden Gate Park, James Turrell's sky-watching subterranean dome at the de Young Museum's sculpture garden is an earth temple or grotto. Genovese architect Renzo Piano's living roof for the Academy of

Sciences, and the San Francisco Museum of Modern Art sculpture garden by Jensen & Macy Architects in collaboration with CMG Landscape Architecture, with its vertical wall garden, are both a return to nature in new—yet ancient—ways. These gardens, too, are fertile ground for creation, perception and meditation.

Camptotheca acuminta *Decne, a Chinese medicinal tree.*

The Garden Wall

Detail from a garden wall designed by Ron Lutsko.

San Francisco designer Topher Delaney's contemporary design for an entry garden that doubles as a space for entertaining guests in San Francisco's Nob Hill is based on the timeless paradise garden.

Eight-foot-high walls surround the 400-square-foot courtyard paved with pale Jerusalem limestone, shielding it from the street. Sliding panels of stainless steel by Larissa Sand conceal an outdoor kitchen pocketed into the east wall.

Free of fussy beds and pots, this garden seems larger and, as tranquil as an Islamic *charbagh*, appropriate for clients who wanted a private enclave in the middle of a busy urban space. Instead of adding intersecting channels of water literally dividing the space into four squares, Delaney created the illusion of water channels where walls and floor meet. She filled narrow troughs for fluorescent lighting with crushed windshield

ABOVE: An entry courtyard has become an urban oasis designed by Topher Delaney, with Jerusalem limestone paving and a high blue plaster wall hand troweled by Terra Briosa in San Francisco.
RIGHT: The walls enclose an outdoor kitchen that can be closed off. In the center is a trough fountain with a tilted Persian-style *chadar* marble panel from India, backed by a mirror to reflect light.

glass. And because the garden is cut off from views of the Golden Gate bay, clearly visible from the house, Delaney chose to simulate water on the garden walls as well.

Designers Tania Saderi, Erin Lilly and Delaney each experimented with shades of gray and blue to create a Mondrianesque seascape, which was rendered in thin plaster veneers over a grid of aluminum strips by artisans from Terra Briosa, a San Francisco company. Blue gray and purple panels shimmer like Persian tile.

A nineteenth-century marble *chadar* cascade from a Mughal building in India, set angled back in a stainless steel frame over a Jerusalem limestone trough, adds a more conventional water feature. Its mirror back reflects a bed of sedum growing in its base. A fragrant mock-orange *Pittosporum undulatum* planted near the fountain and *Juncus patens* marsh grasses and rushes that spring from small openings in the paving complete the blue green mirage in this south-facing urban oasis.

FACING: Stainless steel doors by Larissa Sand in San Francisco slide in a floor groove. Where walls and floor meet, a lighting channel is filled with recycled windshield glass. BELOW: Water washes down the *chadar* face carved with a fish pattern. Water-loving marsh grasses and sedum are grown around it.

CONVERSATION PIECES
BERNARD TRAINOR'S WALLS ARE LOW ENOUGH TO SIT ON

Marie and Geoffrey Moore's garden, behind their 1970s ranch house in the Los Altos hills, was designed by Monterey's Bernard Trainor. His modernist interpretation of Roman stone furniture and short or tall freestanding walls, reminiscent of outdoor partitions by Mexican architect Luis Barragan, punctuate the half-acre space. The "walled" garden is divided into discrete sections: a lowered terrace for a swimming pool; a serenity gravel garden with a bronze water basin that reflects the sky and low, undulating hand-troweled concrete walls that can seat nearly twenty people; and a strolling garden with flagstone walkways interspersed with a planned wilderness of carex, New Zealand and native grasses.

A stand of elms, planted by Thomas Church in the 1950s, provides portals between the gravel-covered Zen-style spaces and the wilderness while a screen of Brazilian hardwood slats mounted on a steel frame is an elegant, friendly barrier at the edge of the property. The resolutely Mediterranean plant palette includes silvery red rosemary, lavender, miniature olives, kalanchoe in custom concrete pots, and mature olive and madrona trees that thrive in the warmth of the northern California peninsula but also contrast pleasingly with the solid snaking walls in this California Eden.

BELOW: Higher walls shield the pool but, visible on the left, a slatted Ipe wood fence lets in light.
RIGHT: Monterey designer Bernard Trainor has incorporated low stucco walls as dividers and seats in a long Los Altos garden. A bowl fountain adds to this gravel-covered "Serenity" garden.
FOLLOWING SPREAD: The gravel area yields to a planned wilderness where carex, native and New Zealand grasses thrive. Red flagstone paths skirt elms originally planted by Thomas Church.

MEXICO IN SANTA MONICA
WALLS TO ECHO THOSE BY ARCHITECT LUIS BARRAGAN

When landscape gardener Joseph Marek heads toward his back garden, he literally gets to work. His office, attached to the main house, overlooks a courtyard-style, half-acre garden, where he experiments with plants against the painted backdrops of buildings that abut his property. That's where he or his partner, John Bernatz, who maintains the garden, can be found when Marek is not at the drawing board or supervising garden installations for clients in the Los Angeles area. People come to him for every style of garden, from traditional English and Spanish to modern, and he has worked as far north as Carmel and Woodside.

Marek is part Mexican and a protégé of Nancy Powers. He left the East Coast, where he went to school, for the West Coast when he came to work for Powers. On his own turf, Marek's taste for bright colors manifests itself in hot pink, deep raspberry, curry and sherbet walls—like those in the architecture of Mexican architect Luis Barragan—that set off foliage and flowers to effect.

Bright color, Marek finds, is calming. His office is painted apricot yellow and his desks are lime green. In Connecticut, where he used to live, that would not have worked, but in "Miami West," this Mexican palette seems entirely at home.

Plants, walls and even outdoor furniture and hanging lanterns are taken into consideration when Marek plans a garden because in Southern California people can really take advantage of life outdoors. Amid seven different sections of his garden—a relatively subdued entry garden with

LEFT: Landscape architect Joseph Marek "borrows" a neighbor's wall as a richly painted backdrop for his own garden in Santa Monica. It obviates the need to raise his own walls to create a courtyard effect, which in this case is "roofed" over by a Chinese elm. The design of the furniture-filled outdoor "rooms" he and his partner, John Bernatz, build and maintain together reflect Marek's Mexican heritage and his penchant for bright colors. Plants are, however, a mix of types selected for texture rather than to evoke regional color. Spanish lavender, New Zealand flaxes, hybrid tea roses, bird-of-paradise plants and a variety of bromeliads including myriad tillandsias abound in this exuberant garden that relies as much on potted specimens—like outdoor house-plants—as it does on perennials planted in the ground.

lavender-, yellow- and white-flowering plants, an entry court-yard with flagstone paving set in a checkerboard pattern, and a fountain in back—Marek planned a dining room and living spaces amid vegetable and cutting flower gardens, where a Chinese elm acts like a roof, and hedges form walls.

Flea-market finds arranged in the beds are as eclectic as Marek's plant selections that bloom at different times of year. Roses in the last week of May start off the flowering season, and in August, coleus, cannas and ginger plants, and in November and December, yellow-blooming aloes are in full flower.

LEFT: A patch of lawn is bordered by a "wall" of succulents pre-dominated by showy 'Sharkskin' agaves, crowned by olive trees.
ABOVE: Marek's flagstone stairway leads to the front door, past more agaves, New Zealand flaxes and bulbs, some of which are potted.

GARDEN AT BIG SUR

WALLS OF LOCAL STONE AND A VIEW OF THE OCEAN

This vast seventy-five-acre oceanside property spreads inland from the main house and caretaker's cottage near the edge of the Pacific, but the steep slopes cascading down to the water are where the owners like to spend their time.

Eric and Silvina Blasen, a landscape design team whose Sausalito company, Blasen, has created a variety of urban, wine country and coastal gardens on the West Coast, decided to create a two-acre garden that, from the air, looks like a quilted blanket on the ground.

They followed the natural contours of the site and outlined sections with walls of native rock and rubble and filled them in with swaths of lavender, native grasses and oleas. Drawings help, but such a garden has to be built organically, and a team of eight stonemasons working

LEFT AND ABOVE: The "hanging" garden Eric and Silvina Blasen designed in Big Sur accommodates the foggy coastal site and its need for hardy low-water plants such as a variety of lavenders like *Lavandula* × *intermedia* 'Grosso', and salvias such as *Salvia leucantha* and *Salvia leucophylla* 'Point Sal'. Stacked-stone retaining walls and carefully crafted stairways by stonemason and sculptor Edwin Hamilton add powerful, beautiful lines to this garden.

with Edwin Hamilton fashioned walls piece by piece. Where the garden peters out, its edges are deliberately planted with more grasses and seeded with wildflowers to seamlessly mesh into the landscape. Stone steps lead down from the house to the ocean nearly 400 feet below.

Because natural springs are abundant on the site, the Blasens were free to plant what they liked but, conscious of the environmental impact of introducing nonnative species, they cordoned off heather, which the owners desired, on a green roof with special acidic soil rather than putting it in the alkaline ground.

The garden is large, but the Blasens wanted a humanistic scale throughout, so walls by Hamilton are deliberately low. Instead of six-foot drops that would have meant fewer walls, the walls are made just high enough to sit on and take in the view.

BELOW: A view of the steep oceanside garden from the top shows its logic clearly. A lawn is bordered by modern stone benches. RIGHT: Instead of a series of steep steps to the ocean, the Blasens designed a garden with gently sloping stairways that lead to plateaus for gatherings. Retaining walls with naturalistic stonework are also low enough to sit on. OVERLEAF: The Blasens' walled garden in the context of its rugged California site, with native sequoias and redwoods.

Aconitum napellus, *a flower used in homeopathy.*

Water in the Garden

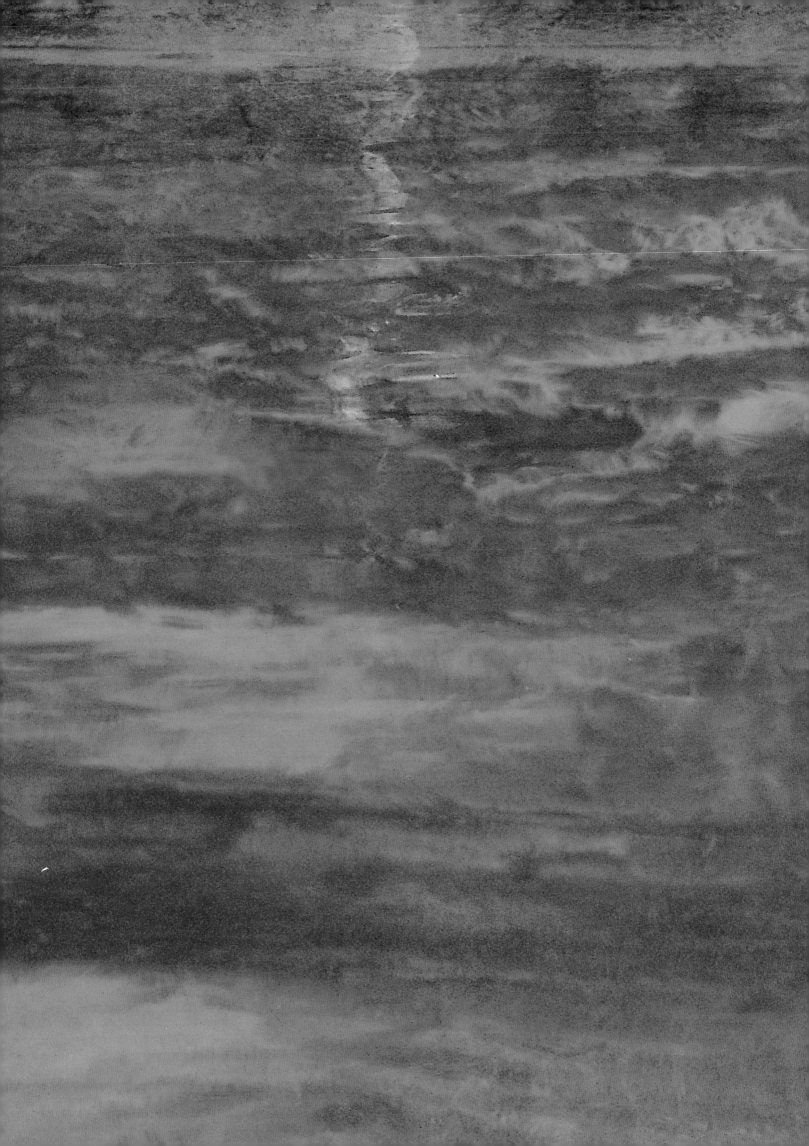

A CRATER LAKE
LOTUS BLOSSOMS IN A WINE COUNTRY POND

Winery owner Betty O'Shaughnessy's favorite spot away from her home in Minnesota was a man-made pond in Oakville, where she had planted lotus and water lilies. For nearly a decade she visited the blossoming vista until it was time to move to it year-round. Her house, designed by architect Ugo Sap, was on the edge of the pond and had large picture windows to take in the vista, but the endless flat views of sixty acres of vines had a downside. They made her beautiful exotic lotus and koi-filled pond seem puny, a blip in the landscape.

Enter landscape architect and steel artist Jack Chandler. He decided to surround the viticultural pond—a round tank of water with nothing else beside

LEFT AND ABOVE: A pond used for irrigation in the wine country around Oakville was planted with lilies long before it was decided to make the site into a cohesive garden. Owner Betty O'Shaughnessy hired sculptor and landscape designer Jack Chandler to transform it. He suggested ringing the pond—which tended to blend in with the vineyards beyond it—with a frame of redwoods and sequoias and a weeping willow tree that flails about dramatically in the wind.

it—with a frame of trees and shrubbery. Chandler moved mounds of earth to create a promontory that juts into the water and planted a swaying willow tree as kinetic sculpture. A group of tall redwoods followed. Boulders along the edge of the pond are intended to make the round pond seem more crater-like, and paths bordered by grasses, irises and roses are seasonal highlights around the crater.

By interrupting the view, Chandler has enhanced it. Fragmented vistas stitched back in the mind's eye form a clearer view. Fences, hedges and low walls provide a comfortable sense of enclosure in most gardens, but at such a large scale, Chandler found trees could serve the same purpose.

The formerly flat, dimensionless pool now has tall shapes reflected on its surface, making it seem deeper. And the trees force the eye to linger at the water's edge and to look at the lotus garden in dappled light.

LEFT: A hot-air balloon comes into view near the pond, where Chandler has given O'Shaugnessy a mass of irises and bushes laden with roses that are regularly gathered for her table. The tree reflections make the pond seem deeper than it really is, adding to its effect. ABOVE: A new gravel-covered walking path that circles the pond is lined with grasses, and boulders are arranged to seem like naturalistic outcroppings. OVERLEAF: An overview of the pond in the last light, when the sun burnishes the water into a molten gold color, all framed by trees and the walking path.

A TASTE OF THE WILD

JOHN SCHARFFENBERGER'S GARDEN IS ABOUT CULTIVATING THE SENSES

John Scharffenberger, an avid naturalist and former vintner and chocolate maker, acquired several acres of land and a coveted redwood grove in the Anderson Valley. To enhance and preserve it, he has carefully thinned some young redwoods, a process called "revirginizing," and created an artificial pond at the edge of the woods. Rampant yellow lotus, papyrus, irises, wildflowers, black oak, maple and alder are encouraged to grow in place of runaway tan oak.

In this vast water garden—which was also the source of material for Scharffenberger's nearby rammed-earth Tuscan-style home—birds, frogs, herons and egrets have taken residence. Many small animals are drawn every day to the pond, and Scharffenberger welcomes the congregation, but it also

ABOVE: Allium from John Scharffenberger's kitchen garden in the Anderson Valley. RIGHT: Amid redwood groves, a viticultural pond—kept algae free with blue dye—attracts birds and frogs.

means that a *potager* near the kitchen has to be surrounded by a high earthen wall and gate to keep out these visitors.

Inside the boundaries of this smaller garden, Scharffenberger indulges his taste for vegetables, rosemary, *Salvia sclarea* (clary sage), *Macleaya cordata,* sedum, angelica, glowing dogwood and a collection of exotic plants that might seem odd in the riparian habitat he has created. Tidy beds edged with boxwood and teucrium contain a mix that includes low geraniums, and *Gunnera tinctoria* grows beside redwood stumps, from the time the area was logged in the 1880s. Garden peas, arugula, broccoli, cabbage, bok choy, leeks, onions, lettuces, cucumbers, tomatoes and squash provide a mélange of seasonal textures and, like the frequent visitors attracted to the pond, friends are drawn to Scharffenberger's table.

LEFT: Beds bordered with clipped boxwood or teucrium contain a merry mix of rosemary and other ornamental herbs, glowing dogwood, sedum, salvias, garden peas, rampant yellow lotus, papyrus, arugula, broccoli and leeks. ABOVE: Close to the naturalistic pond amid the forest, dug in part to supply mud for Scharffenberger's rammed-earth Tuscan villa, a garden gate opens into a walled potager that is laid out in a formal Mediterranean style.

GREEN ROOMS
BRINGING LIGHT INTO AN OVERGROWN ST. HELENA ESTATE GARDEN

After several years in Hawaii, Dick and Monene Bradley moved to a sixty-acre estate in St. Helena developed during the nineteenth century by gold and silver baron William Bourn, whose son built the 1917 Filoli Estate in Woodside.

It had been used as a retreat for the Christian Brothers Winery, and driveways, wire fences and other additions—not part of the original design—were visually jarring and undermined the bones of the original garden. Another unfortunate alteration, probably from the 1960s, was a semicircle of grass with a border of cracked concrete around the swimming pool. Old pines, redwoods and oaks grew, untended, right up to the edge of the pool.

Garden designer Bob Clark and landscape architect Ralph Barnes helped the couple revive parts of the original design with several changes that also contemporize it.

They removed nearly forty of the old trees that made the garden feel dark and crowded, and replaced them with Japanese maples for seasonal bursts of color and light. New pergolas and arbors make better canopies than the old trees did and allow outdoor living in hot wine country summers.

Paths bordered by plants link these "rooms" together. Clark prefers textured gardens with dense painterly plantings in the English style that the Bradleys, who are originally from the East Coast, also favor.

Around the pool, which Clark has tried to make more pondlike, *Equisetum hyemale,* a reed, is planted in sculptural clumps. Lush plants like these with brighter greens and strong textures hold their own within the formal framework of the old garden. The juxtaposition of new and old is a recurring theme. Bradford pear and cherry trees were combined with mature oaks and pines, further anchored to the site with underplantings of hydrangeas and euphorbia, contrasted with oak leaf lettuce, yellow narcissus, and *Berberis thunbergii atropurpurea.* Bronze and green fennel make pleasing contrasts for the most part, but Clark relied on soft foliage and forms to make the strongly classical original a unified composition in several shades of green dappled with light.

LEFT: When garden designer Bob Clark was confronted with a classic formal frame at the late nineteenth-century garden his clients wanted to renovate, he decided to clear away overgrown trees and pines—redwoods and oaks that had encroached into a circular lawn area around the swimming pool. He removed a number of the trees, planted low Japanese maples and built arbors for climbing vines close to the pool. The arbors provide shade and a sense of outdoor rooms. Around the pool he added stone paving in place of the old cracked concrete, and to make the pool more pondlike, he added a clump of *Equisetum hyemale*, a water-loving reed, that also brings a fresh, modern touch to the design.

LEARNING THEIR LINES

A TEXAS COUPLE IN EUGENE, OREGON, DISCOVER THE JOY OF RAIN

A little information is all you need to get hooked into gardening in the Northwest, as Buell Steelman and Rebecca Sams, a couple from Texas who moved to Eugene, Oregon, found out.

They had studied liberal arts and immersed themselves in the classics, but their first jobs at Gardens, a design/build landscape architecture firm in Austin, Texas, threw them into a crash course in design and gardening. At the end of it, they knew much about dry gardens, but in Eugene, the speed at which things grew was another learning curve.

Nonetheless, the experience they'd had in building the bones of a good garden helped them to launch their new design/build business—Garden Mosaic—and to revive known garden forms that would contain this new-found cornucopia. At home, it helped them to get things in line, literally, with strict retaining walls of basalt stone, straight paths and beds brimming with colorful pineapple lily, *Eucomis comosa* 'Sparkling Burgundy', lacy heuchera and bright blue noble fir.

ABOVE: The stone stairway to Rebecca Sams and Buell Steelman's home and garden showcases their use of plants for textured, painterly effects. RIGHT: The garden wraps around all sides of the house, connected by a series of straight stone and gravel paths that lead to destinations such as this water garden in a galvanized tub. OVERLEAF: Sams and Steelman's full gamut of color.

On their sloping one-acre lot where front, side and rear gardens wrap around the house, the stages in which visitors see each space are controlled. So Steelman and Sams decided to allot a different use to each space—flower, water and kitchen gardens, and at the end, an orchard—and linked them together with a series of narrow stone and gravel paths that come to circular openings to showcase sculpture or showy urns. This nod to French and Italian gardens of the Renaissance seems fresh because of its comfortable scale and their use of contemporary low-cost materials such as a shiny galvanized stock tank for a water garden filled with a hardy lily, *Nymphaea* 'Virginalis', and a wood-and-steel deck on stilts that overlooks the orchard for alfresco dining. Ancient rooftop gardens of the Middle East, the Italian loggia and French landscape architect André Le Nôtre's tricks with perspective are all here. And if the helter-skelter, joyous mix of plants they could never have before gets unruly, they'll just clip away. That, they know how to do.

LEFT To sit and enjoy their central water feature, Steelman and Sams have added a curved slab bench, hidden within the beds. ABOVE Elsewhere in the garden, where they have an outdoor grill of stone, a terrace raised on stilts has potted bamboo and a place for alfresco dining.

A GARDEN IN THE WOODS
REFLECTING ON NATURE MEANS KEEPING THINGS SIMPLE

Architect Olle Lundberg, designer of Larry Ellison's Pacific Heights home in San Francisco, Rudd Winery and several other wine country estates, is not averse to salvaging whatever his clients no longer need.

When a water tank from a defunct cattle farm came available, the rugged Nordic architect wanted it for use as a *frigidarium* in his Napa Valley property. The sixteen-foot round redwood tank was so large it had to be taken apart and reassembled on-site piece by piece. Lundberg found a ridge close to his house, cut a pad at its foot and poured a concrete foundation to tuck the tank snug against the hillside. The rotted top of the tank had to be shaved off, which was fine because it lowered the tank by two feet—just the right height to run a redwood ramp from the back of the house to the tank. The long, narrow deck is a runway when Lundberg emerges from a hot tub inset into the deck and makes a beeline for the bracing water in his new fourteen-foot-deep infinity circle that reflects his natural garden of live oaks, redwoods and the moon.

LEFT AND BELOW Architect Olle Lundberg's weekend hideout in Napa Valley, north of San Francisco, has a recycled water tank he uses as a cold-plunge pool. A new hot tub is just yards away.

A WATERFRONT GARDEN

A MODEL SEATTLE GARDEN ON THE EDGE OF A CANAL

A 1925 farmhouse on six acres of land beside the Hood Canal outside Seattle was ideal for Nancy Heckler, an editor with *Martha Stewart* magazine who grew up in Illinois and was ready for more than flat land. She had always wanted a farm with a barn, and her former husband, Terry, an artist, wanted to be near the water.

A bluff overlooks the beach, and on the east side you can see the Olympic Mountains in the background. This lucky find, over a decade ago, led to one of the most elaborate series of gardens spread over two acres, connected by paths and arbors that took the place of cherry and apple orchards overrun with blackberries.

Heckler removed some trees and replaced others in the same grid but kept the gnarly old plum trees intact. New meandering paths reveal each section gradually, giving the impression of a much larger estate garden. A rose garden, a woodland garden, a tropical garden and a decorative vegetable garden all merge one into the next, making it a giant discovery garden. Woven cedar fencing and embellishments such as an enormous nest tucked within the undergrowth are hidden treats to chance upon.

RIGHT: Nancy Heckler's Hood Canal garden has a vegetable plot you enter through a vine-covered arbor flanked by lavender. Besides vegetables, the plot's borders brim with dark foliage such as *Phormium* 'Dark Delight', a New Zealand flax, and dark-leaved dahlias. BELOW A large nest sculpture is the kind of surprise Heckler conceals along paths leading to the water's edge.

Woodland orchids, Martagon lilies and large swaths of colorful flowering plants are floated under very large Douglas fir trees with huge trunks that have been limbed and thinned to let in light. The effect is naturalistic, the way Heckler prefers a garden.

It is a showcase of what a temperate climate with plenty of rain allows: Heckler can grow almost everything year-round, and she can naturalize bulbs or leave perennials like dahlias in the ground through the winter.

The only thing she has to be concerned about is excessive water and proper drainage. When water percolates down to a bed of clay a couple of feet under the topsoil, it settles in for the winter. Plants don't like that, and Heckler is the first to hear about it.

LEFT AND ABOVE: Bark-covered paths lead to the Hood Canal's edge in Heckler's garden. Lacy silver artemesia, upright golden ornamental grass, old-fashioned shrub roses, tree peonies and even hardy tropical banana trees, orchids and lilies are planted in a melange so naturalistically that they seem to belong in this landscape.

WATER GARDEN
A PARADISE GARDEN IN THE WINE COUNTRY

For Ron Lutsko, a professional sailor turned landscape designer in San Francisco, open meadows full of irises—that resemble oceans—and water features are essential while designing a garden.

At the LEF Foundation, a philanthropic arts organization and gallery in Napa Valley, he created a didactic garden that underscores the role of water in a viticultural estate.

Existing buildings on the property, including a stone winery, a barn and a cooperage, had been converted into the founder's home, an office, a gallery and a retreat for visiting artists and guests.

The gardens Lutsko designed around them are expansive or intimate, to indicate whether the buildings were for public or private use.

Since these gardens were part of an arts complex, an entry courtyard on the northeast side outside the foundation's offices was designed to be a space for exhibiting sculpture—presided over by a permanent stone installation by artist Andy Goldsworthy.

The west side of the estate became the domestic landscape—a loose interpretation of a paradise garden—with the swimming pool standing in for the

LEFT A drawbridge from a raised section of the garden leads to the residence above the gallery.
BELOW An example of concrete fountains Lutsko designed, with water circulating through them.

garden's symbolic reflecting pond, surrounded by lawns and vegetable and cutting gardens.

On the eastern edge of the three-acre property, where it slopes toward the Napa River, an orchard of espaliered figs surrounds a man-made, grass-covered mound. The mound is covered with rare *Calamagrostis foliosa,* a federally protected plant; the mound echoes hills in the distance but, more importantly, acts as a buffer when the river swells to overflowing each winter. From the mound, a drawbridge leads up to the second-floor entry to the residence.

Elsewhere, trellised areas and a grove of olive trees provide shade.

For the most part, the style of the garden is not formal but agrarian, with tough steel and wire fencing, stone and concrete dividers, and galvanized sheathing around garden structures.

Simple concrete or stone water channels and fountains—like those in Islamic gardens—allude to the river nearby but also link the deliberately disparate sections. A galvanized pipe puts well water into a long, thin concrete channel eleven inches wide that runs through most of the site.

When the water rill has to be interrupted to make way for bridgeless paths, a line of limestone pavers marks the water trail. The pavers "flow" under the

LEFT: The swimming pool serves as the central water feature in this complicated paradise garden.
ABOVE: Beds of tulips and flowering cherry trees provide seasonal color in this garden, which is mostly a study in greens. The concrete rills slow when they intersect with paths and entryways but continue on the other side either as similar channels or just strips of flagstone paving that depict the water line connecting the different public and private sections of the garden.

entry drawbridge that is made of grating, so light spills through to accent the kinetic, "watery" thread below.

Closer to the house, cooling sculptural water features—cascades flowing down stainless steel screens through which vineyards are visible, or articulated waterfalls flowing over polished cut limestone—are visible reminders of more private space.

Colorful flowers are beautiful, Lutsko maintains during his lectures at UC Berkeley, where he teaches landscape architecture, but they are not essential, especially in California. Swaths of green and blue to counter brown hills are more exciting. Expanses of grass or even stone and gravel rather than spotty colorful compositions are important, he says. When possible, a background wall of color is used to simply highlight foliage. At the LEF garden, Lutsko's ideas are derived from cultural and ecological links to the landscape, compartmentalized as carefully as vineyards or fields.

ABOVE: A custom-galvanized gate on wheels rolls into place to cordon off the LEF gallery entrance and courtyard from the rest of the estate. RIGHT: A brilliant blue plaster wall—like a cascade of water—demarcates the gallery office building. Limestone pavers and flowering redbud trees add a modern Zen quality to the garden.

RIVERS OF ROCK
A SONOMA GARDEN OVERFLOWS WITH STONE

A financier who grew up on a ranch, and his wife, an interior designer, acquired bits of their seventeen-acre Stone Edge estate in Glen Ellen, Sonoma County, over many years. Each time they added more land, the couple could indulge in several more different kinds of gardens, including a working farm with vineyards, full-grown Manzanillo olive groves, orchards with Roma apple and pear trees and vegetable beds. Wild grasses and lavender planted in neat rows establish a grid to stitch the disparate pieces together.

Their olive oil is now sold in San Francisco stores and the wine is aging, but the property's defining product seems to be stone, and each of the many landscape designers who have worked on this ongoing garden have found ample use for it.

Topher Delaney and Andrea Cochran have each contributed designs with walls and stepped terraces here and

ABOVE: An archway of local stone leads into Glen Ellen's Stone Edge estate, which is part winery and part olive farm. A creek that runs through it seasonally helps to irrigate the property.
RIGHT: The creek bed, between olive groves and vineyards, was lined with stone and straightened by Roger Warner, who also planted its banks with clipped balls of lavender.

there, but Roger Warner used the stone to unify the entire property.

Warner planned stone paths that now link several structures—a refurbished shed where olive oil is stored, a dining pergola and the main house. A gateway at the entrance, columns for an octagonal arbor and even a stone table under it are fashioned from local stone. V-shaped runnels of field stone divert winter streams efficiently, but Warner also likes a more natural look (near the front door, he has a bowl hollowed out in a huge boulder to catch dew from a tree), so, rock by rock, he re-created naturalistic dry creek beds meandering through the garden, as if it were a plein air painting of the real thing.

LEFT AND ABOVE: More archways laden with ornamental gourds or flowering vines lead to other sections of the garden. Holes in the stone steps, above, become flower pots for herbs or medicinal plants.
BELOW: A hollowed-rock birdbath is fed by dew drops from overshadowing plants.
OVERLEAF: In one section, Warner decided to re-create the original creek bed as naturalistically as possible.

Echinacea paradoxa, *an herbal flower used medicinally.*

Dry Gardens

LIVING WITH CACTUS

TWO COLLECTORS ADMIRE THE ARCHITECTURAL BEAUTY OF SUCCULENTS

Margaret Majua, a trained horticulturist, and her partner, architect David Weingarten of Ace Architects, have a shapely but prickly cactus and succulent garden surrounding their early-California-style 1928 house on a ten-acre estate in Lafayette.

Weingarten—a nephew of architect Charles Moore and known for his joyous structures that take the shape of dragons and fantastic creatures that invite play—elected not to change the house but instead chose the garden as a playground.

The old garden simply didn't suit their hacienda-style home, so Weingarten and Majua removed offending pine trees too close to the house, roses and other plants that seemed out of place. Old wisteria and beds of iris were saved from the hatchet, partly because they were out of the way, and because they provided seasonal color.

Finding sources for cactus to plant in beds proved harder than they thought because growers and stores typically provide full-grown ornamental specimens in pots. The Bay Area's other cactus ground gardens—the UC Botanical Garden, parts of the Arboretum in San Francisco, and Ruth Bancroft's famous

LEFT: A vintage wisteria vine is just one of the few things Margaret Majua and architect David Weingarten saved of the original garden at their Lafayette home, which is now surrounded by a cactus garden they culled at nurseries such as Grisby Cactus Gardens near San Diego and the Great Petaluma Desert in Sonoma. ABOVE: 'Century Plant' agaves line the driveway up to the house.

Walnut Creek garden—became their libraries even though they all have more succulents and arid plants than cactus. The couple eventually discovered sources—Grigsby Cactus Gardens near San Diego, and the Great Petaluma Desert in Sonoma—to get their garden going.

The ground was reshaped—and backfilled with porous rock and little organic material—so the slope of the hillside garden was exaggerated. Things looked good until the first winter decimated most of the plants they chose, except, they found out later, the ones that were accustomed to higher elevations and frost.

For the kind of color most gardeners want, Weingarten and Majua found night-blooming cactus. Red, yellow, chartreuse and white blossoms such as *Trichocereus* hybrids are prickly but beautiful.

Saguaro, the ubiquitous desert plant in cowboy movies, branched *Cereus* and *Trichocereus*, as well as several species of popular broad-leaved *Opuntia* are now acclimated to their setting. Spiky *Opuntia ficus-indica* bears seductive yellow flowers and edible fruit and is not as unfriendly as it seems. It is the tiny spines of *Opuntia santa-rita* that are less visible and therefore more lethal.

Plants in their driveway are more welcoming. Palms, flowering aloes and rows of succulent 'Century Plant' agaves that have deep roots but rarely flower, are all showy, softer and sculptural in this new desertscape.

BELOW AND RIGHT: Around the house, saguaro cactus, like the kind seen in cowboy movies, branched *Cereus* and *Trichocereus,* and broad-leaved *Opuntia* require a lot of care even if they need hardly any water. Amid the wisteria and scilla saved from the former garden, the spiky cactuses take on a softer air. OVERLEAF: Cactus plants such as *Trichocereus* hybrids flower profusely too.

THE THRILL OF EUPHORBIA
A SUCCULENT GARDEN TO LIVE BY

For decades, the life-affirming process of growing indestructible, madly multiplying clusters of evergreen euphorbia has absorbed Dr. Herman Schwartz, a retired oncologist who used to treat children dying of leukemia. A botanist long before he became a doctor, Schwartz was drawn to a book on succulents by the German botanist Werner Rauh and began to build a collection of plants. When he retired from medicine, he returned full time to an undying passion for euphorbia, and wrote nearly twenty books of his own, including *Euphorbia Journal* and *The History of Succulents*.

As these books will tell you, euphorbia and cactuses are both spiny desert plants, with many characteristics in common. Principally, they can each withstand erratic moisture conditions, and one enterprising type of euphorbia even has roots that go down 100 feet to get water. But while cactuses are also succulents, not all succulents are cactuses. The difference lies in the ways they propagate with or without flowers and seeds.

ABOVE: Dr. Herman Schwartz's greenhouse, a simple shed with plastic roofing, is command central at his Bolinas euphorbia treasure house. RIGHT: In the meadow where he has successfully acclimated many kinds of euphorbia from around the world, he reserves an area for children to grow plants.

LEFT AND ABOVE: *Philodendron bipinnatifidum* (syn. *Philodendron selloum*) and red-flowering *Euphorbia milli* that won't grow well in cold northern California conditions grow inside Schwatz's greenhouse. OVERLEAF: These succulents grow readily in Schwartz's meadow.

As his knowledge grew with his collection, Schwartz bought sixteen acres in Bolinas, next to the Niman hog and cattle ranch, and extended the original horse barn on the property to include greenhouses, so he could observe samples gathered in their natural habitats around the world during California winters. Many suffered in a cooler climate but they all lived. These euphorbia factories—perhaps unnecessary when you consider their indestructible nature—supply Schwartz's sprawling garden with hundreds of species gathered from Africa, India, South America, Central America and the United States. His private garden is now the Marin Bolinas Botanical Garden. On an acre set aside in his living museum garden, Schwartz invites children to harvest samples and see his miracle plant for themselves. Every child who visits gets to keep a fantastic euphorbia.

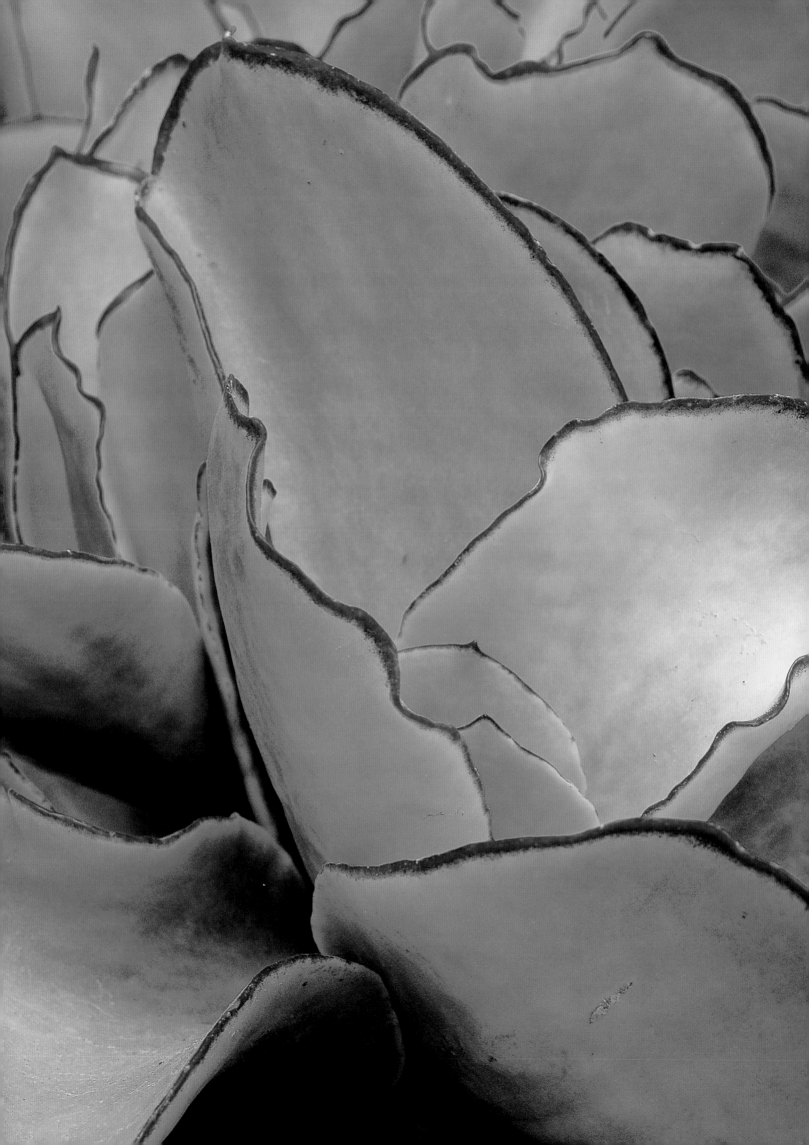

A SOUTHERN CALIFORNIA PALETTE

PATRICK ANDERSON'S WONDERFUL WORLD OF SUCCULENTS

In Fallbrook, California, a tiny township north of San Diego near Mt. Palomar, Patrick Anderson's giant succulents on a two-acre hillside thrust skyward, in a complementary display of orange blossoms against blue sky.

As if that were not enough, a twelve-foot-long freestanding wall painted a brilliant cobalt blue stands in the west side of the garden, throwing more shapes and blossoms into high relief in this sculptural succulent garden.

Anderson, a collector since he was just ten, has accumulated more than a thousand stunning varieties of New World agaves, large tree aloes and low-growing clumping types from Africa, euphorbias in diverse forms and shapes and lately an increasing number of true cactuses. For textural variety, he has interspersed perennials such as native poppies among his prized collection and desert palms that require the same soil and weather conditions.

Anderson's partner, Lester Olson, a retired judge, was enlisted to build and supervise each aspect of the garden, which has evolved over several years

LEFT AND BELOW: A blue wall is the perfect backdrop for flowering succulents in Patrick Anderson's version of the Huntington Botanical Gardens at his home near San Diego. Stone steps lead up to the top of the hilly site and low footbridges cross over a simulated creek bed.

from a steep, sloping, rock-less orchard of unwanted lime trees into a boulder-strewn arrangement of asphalt and winding pea gravel paths that circle up to a yellow tile-roofed loggia they built as a place to entertain friends. Water gullies disguised as dry creek beds filled with riverine rock cascade down the hillside.

When it rains hard, and it rarely does, Olson and Anderson are prepared with channels to direct the water into the creek beds, and just for kicks, Olson has built a couple of low footbridges to cross them. The only thing they dread now is frost, which turns water-rich succulents to icicles. Lucky for them, that happens rarely too.

In such dry terrain, a succulent garden seems the obvious choice, but Anderson's fascination for the varieties he has planted deepened when he lived in Los Angeles and volunteered at the Huntington Botanical Gardens. In Fallbrook, he has replicated that famous desert garden—and in some ways reinvented it with painterly drifts and swaths of golden barrel cactuses—and thrills in its riot of vibrant color every January when the garden blooms.

ABOVE: Golden barrel cactuses, the Huntington Gardens' ninety-five-year-old signature plant, also thrive in Anderson's garden. RIGHT: A yellow stucco and clay tile pavilion at the highest point of the garden is where he and partner Lester Olson entertain guests when the cactus garden is in bloom. OVERLEAF: A wide view of Anderson and Olson's textural masterpiece.

HIGH AND DRY IN THE CITY

A PENTHOUSE SUCCULENT GARDEN

When architect Maria McVarish recon-figured the high-ceilinged penthouse loft in a former shirt factory, ballet school and warehouse as a space with a grove of freestanding rooms on stilts, she wanted an equally adventurous gar-den for the adjoining roof terrace.

Landscape designer Andrea Cochran, noted for her crisp abstract work, has designed a succulent garden in long wavy tubs of steel laid side by side a few feet apart. The abstract seascape suits McVarish's interior design and contrasts effectively with the urban

LEFT AND BELOW: Andrea Cochran has designed an orderly landscape of undulating hills covered with native grasses and succulents in a flat penthouse garden in San Francisco's Hayes Valley. The "hills" are galvanized steel tubs surrounded by river rock and boardwalks of Trex compos-ite decking. An orange steel-and-Lucite wall sculpture by Lawrence LaBianca screens off neighbors.
OVERLEAF: At night, fiber-optic lights embedded in the walkways lead the way.

setting dominating the skyline beyond the innovative garden.

The textures and colors in the tubs are deliberate, painterly selections. Trex composite decking covers most of the terrace, and at night, strips of dramatic fiber-optic lights embedded in the decking lead the way around the tubs. The many reflective surfaces merge the lit garden into the cityscape at night.

The Hayes Valley neighborhood in San Francisco is sunny but sometimes windy, so McVarish commissioned a sculptural screen by San Francisco artist Lawrence LaBianca along the east wall to shield her south-facing garden from wind as well as to gain privacy. On the west side, a canopy, also by LaBianca, provides a place to relax in a protected garden room.

ABOVE: Flared steel pots, also Cochran's design, along LaBianca's sculpture wall, contain more succulents. RIGHT: On the opposite side of the garden, LaBianca created a steel-and-Lucite canopy that provides a shielded place to sit and read. A wire-and-wood railing above a projecting bay in the building façade is the spot for the best urban views. The building façade is covered in outdoor-grade Finply, a European resin and wood panel first used in San Francisco for this project.

FLASHY WONDERS ON A MOUNTAINTOP

PROTEUS AS SHOWY AS LAS VEGAS GRACES A HILLY SAN DIEGO ESTATE

When Tom Krumholz and his wife, Cindy, retired nearly twenty-six years ago, the former marine from Camp Pendleton and business graduate, who had worked as a sales manager for a large printing company, didn't think he would become a gardener.

But the land they found—seven rocky acres on a hill an hour north of San Diego—had limitless views (on a fine day they can see the Catalina Islands and the ocean thirty miles away) and nothing would grow on it naturally. There was no water up there, and seasonal brush was all the land could support. Eagles, hawks, coyotes, roadrunners and mountain lions didn't mind too much, but less hardy creatures avoided this space.

Krumholz leveled a pad at the top and built a 3,200-square-foot ranch house on it. Rubble dynamited from the hilltop was reused to form a driveway

LEFT AND ABOVE: Tom and Cindy Krumholz's protea garden in the hills around San Diego overlooks their former avocado farms in the valley below. Well-drained soil and dry conditions mitigated on the hottest days by drip irrigation every other day has created an unparalleled protea paradise. Many rare species bloom year-round and none have been affected by frost, a natural enemy of the plant. Large boulders, saved from the site where they built their home atop the hill, look like natural outcroppings the plants like. Many were also embedded into the new driveway.

up to the house. The rest of the land they left alone.

Just ten years ago, with water readily at hand, they began to plant among the rocks and boulders on the site, mainly to stay occupied and to send visitors home with flowers. Proteus, they discovered, not only liked the rocky soil and windswept-but-frostless conditions but also, in April and May, produced the most jaw-dropping blossoms they had ever seen. Besides, in Minnesota, where his family used to live, they could never have had this unique blossom, which dies when the temperature sinks below

freezing. In Valley Center, where the Krumholzes are, they know the mercury never dips that low—thanks to their natural barometers that have never died.

The Krumholzes plant specimens they find in nurseries that propagate rare and unusual varieties, and now over 150 hummingbirds come to investigate their bounty spread over more than two acres. In some seasons, the harvest is so good that they ship it across the country to florists or to use in hotel lobbies as far as Las Vegas. This enterprise certainly pays the water bill for Valhalla.

ABOVE: Silhouetted against the sky, there is nothing more dramatic than a row of agaves, another Krumholz favorite. More than fifty types of spring-blooming cactuses perhaps outnumber the Krumholzes thirty-five varieties of protea, but it is the protea plant that puts their garden on the map. RIGHT: Along a gravel path are more proteas, large evergreen shrubs from South Africa with humdrum foliage but spectacular flowers that resemble extravagant artichokes, pincushions and tubular flowers that are used for bouquets.

A PAINTER'S GARDEN

A SEMI-ARID GARDEN GLOWS ON A STEEP SITE IN MALIBU

Landscape designer Tina Beebe, a student of the artist Josef Albers and for a time a graphic designer associated with Ray Eames, has learned to garden by happenstance. Her grandmothers and her mother were avid gardeners, and Beebe's own fascination with gardens was awakened by a need to paint and perhaps by the subliminal tug of her name, which means beekeeper.

In Santa Monica and later in Malibu, where she and her husband, architect Buzz Yudell, built their home in 1989,

spring became a time to paint English roses and California poppies. The more she painted, the more complex her plant palette grew, and after a decade, the south-facing garden, laid out in a series of terraces linked with steps, is a painter's dream.

The outdoor rooms—an enfilade of walled or hedged courtyards alongside the long downsloping house set parallel to an arroyo on the western side— include an entry court, a trellised stucco colonnade, an allée of pineapple guavas

BELOW: A stepped approach to the top of the site is flanked by the house on the right and Tina Beebe's series of terraced gardens that are each designed as outdoor rooms, with the swimming pavilion up top. RIGHT: An allée of pineapple guava trees and a collonaded stucco arbor lead the way into Tina Beebe's garden in Malibu.

and trellised courtyards off the living spaces and master bedroom that culminate in a draped pavilion by the pool that overlooks the Pacific, a mile away.

A colorist with Moore Ruble Yudell architects, Beebe is now an amateur horticulturist who dots her garden with color groupings like a pointillist painter. New plant combinations are worked out on this large canvas—because a good garden can never be planned fully on paper—getting wilder and more drought tolerant the farther this pavilion garden gets from the house.

LEFT: The terraces, such as this Mediterranean-style walled flagstone court dotted with California poppies, euphorbia and dry weather plants, get more drought resistant the farther they are from the main house. ABOVE AND BELOW: A cabana beside the pool has ocean views.

HOME ON THE BEACH
SUN, SAND AND HOLD THE TURF

Driving north from San Francisco to Stinson Beach, Kim Wright-Violich comes home to glimpses of the ocean. This is the reward Wright-Violich, manager of a charitable fund and the mother of three teenage children, needs every day. At Stinson, warm sand during the summer, a walk on the beach with their two dogs or simply watching the sunset are treats just a few yards away from her front door. It's where her children surf, boogie board or play volleyball and, occasionally, she likes to join them.

Wright-Violich's L-plan, redwood-clad house, designed by Michael Siegel in the 1960s, reflects that era's seminal Sea Ranch houses that used wood siding, raked roofs and boxy shapes. Four decades later, Siegel's work needed repair and Wright-Violich needed more rooms. Architect Peter Pfau helped with an extension that blends into the original rough-sawn redwood siding and barnlike character of the building.

The addition has also created a windshield for the entry courtyard, which is

LEFT: Inside, the Blasens added to existing Trex decking, so it now covers the entire front garden to provide a wider area for outdoor living. Beds are filled with hardy *Stipa ichu* grasses and a blue agave. ABOVE: A compound of aging buildings revived by architect Peter Pfau and landscape designers Eric and Silvina Blasen near Stinson Beach, north of San Francisco, now has a slatted fence and entry gate and raised *Myoporum laetum* 'Carsonii' hedges for privacy.
OVERLEAF: "Camp Stinson" has a boardwalk to an area for guest tents that goes past Mulenbergia rigens deer grass, more *Stipa ichu*, Peruvian feather grass and clumps of *Artemisia schmidtiana* 'Silver Mound' plants.

now, thanks to Sausalito landscape designers Eric and Silvina Blasen, a boardwalk abutting a sandy garden. On sunny mornings and moonlit evenings Wright-Violich has the kind of beach she likes right at her doorstep.

The Blasen's filled in the entire courtyard with composition fiber Trex decking to match an existing wrap-around deck. It makes the courtyard seem bigger and also more practical for dogs and children. Inset planters contain native grasses that thrive and sway in the beach air. Where a lean-to office was removed to make room for a Jacuzzi, the Blasens installed a private contemplative garden with fragrant vines and *Rosa* 'Sombreuil'. New out-door showers outside the garage building and barn doors that open directly from the new master bedroom onto the central space have brought life out into the open.

A poured-concrete fire pit became a focal point of the new deck just outside the new master bedroom, where the family can huddle even on foggy days. Instead of working from drawings, Pfau, the Blasens and the contractor made a model with foam pieces propped in place to determine the right shape and size. In the section of the property that is uncovered, the designers created Camp Stinson, a beach with more sand and grasses, where permanent guest tents gleam like beacons at night.

LEFT: Another collaborative design, the concrete fire pit at the center of the garden, just off the new master bedroom, is a central gathering spot for the entire family. To the left of it is a path to the beach. A boardwalk in the distance leads to guest tents at "Camp Stinson." ABOVE: The concrete-and-slatted-wood front gate and trellis were designed by Blasen and Pfau Architecture.

Datura *flower used in ancient Ayurvedic medicine.*

Pavilions and Follies

A painted steel trellis by Ron Lutsko was built for a vintage wisteria vine.

A PAGODA FANTASY

A NINETEENTH-CENTURY-STYLE FOLLY REPRISED AS A PLACE TO ENTERTAIN

Nan McEvoy of the de Young family, founders of the *San Francisco Chronicle,* retired from the family business to a ranch in Marin County, little expecting to become a farmer.

The goal was simply a return to the country and a lifestyle she knew as a child growing up in Burlingame, south of San Francisco. Pony carts and ice cream vendors aren't exactly circling her city apartment these days, but in the country she felt she could replicate some of her own pastoral suburban childhood for her grandchildren.

To build the home and gardens she wanted also meant cultivating a farm on her property strictly designated as agricultural land. Olives seemed like the least demanding and, spurred by what she read in Maggie Klein's *The Feast of the Olive,* McEvoy began to plant her grove. Within a decade, the trees produced the finest olive oil on the market, and the ranch now attracts a steady stream of enthusiastic visitors.

In this evolving 550-acre *paradeisos* of classical proportions, McEvoy dreamed of a pavilion to host those visitors. Soon, interior designers Babey Moulton Jue & Booth (BAMO) conjured up a forty-two-foot-high Chinese pagoda with giant copper lizards on its roof, because skinks,

BELOW: Lizards, like the native skinks that roam the McEvoy ranch in Marin, have become the olive farm's logo. They were replicated in cast bronze as door handles for the Chinese-style pavilion.
RIGHT: A view of the McEvoy olive groves interspersed with lavender, herb gardens and fruit trees.

real lizards, that lurk among the olives are a source of delight for McEvoy's grandchildren and have become the symbol and logo of the McEvoy ranch.

Michael Booth, in charge of the pavilion design, looked at the Tabernacle, a Methodist center with a delicate silhouette built on Martha's Vineyard in 1879, as a model. Responding also to McEvoy's fondness for chinoiserie, Booth referenced a Chinese teahouse in Rhode Island, at Alva Vanderbilt's Marble House, and created an amalgam of the two to suit the pastoral setting. The result, closer in feeling to the Chinese Tea House at Sans Souci near Berlin, is an octagonal pavilion with wide openings and fits well amid redwoods, olive groves and open hilly terrain.

This elaborate tent, of resawn cedar boards and a pagoda-style roof of copper, will weather naturally to gray and verdigris. Steel doors designed by Jefferson Mack will help to keep out ocean fog. The metal roof required a different kind of smithery, so Booth found Larry Stearns of Vermont, who restores capitol domes, to create copper shingles to replicate clay Chinese tiles. The giant skinks for the roof, according to Booth, were Stearns' idea.

They became so popular with the McEvoys, skink-shaped bronze handles for the doors and wall sconces in the shape of dragons were added inside. In this reptilian fantasy, tile paving and river rock used in pathways in Chinese gardens are embedded in the pavilion floor in a geometric pattern.

Above this showy carpet, interior details are deliberately subtle and yet grand. The ceiling, of beaded boards, is draped like billowing fabric, and the underside of the cupola is painted blue like a patch of sky. Wood and silk lanterns suspended from the ceiling—like oil lamps in Moorish buildings—add a flickering glow to the pavilion—a destination in the vast, sylvan landscape even on foggy nights.

PREVIOUS PAGE: The pagoda-style pavilion designed by Babey Moulton Jue & Booth (BAMO) has more skinks slithering up its copper roof. In the background, the hillsides are covered with olive groves.
LEFT: Newspaper heiress Nan McEvoy's penchant for chinoiserie is fully realized inside her garden pavilion. Its wood-clad ceiling, shaped in billowing folds like a tent canopy, has copper-and-bronze light fittings as well as silk lanterns hanging from it, and the floor, an elaborate mosaic of stone and tile, is derived from Chinese originals.
TOP RIGHT: A patch of ceiling just under the finial is painted blue to resemble the sky. RIGHT: A detail of the stone-and-tile mosaic floor laid as a continuous carpet inside and outside the pavilion. The quatrefoil motif is composed of thin glazed tiles and river rock.

PERENNIAL COLOR IN A FLOWERLESS GARDEN
A HIGH-WATTAGE ART INSTALLATION IN SAN FRANCISCO

Shirley Watts studied art long before she took on a horticultural palette to design artful living installations.

For doctors Sam and Irene Pleasure who live in Sunset, the foggiest section of San Francisco, Watts created a colorful pop composition of gravel beds, boxwood, a water sculpture and a pavilion.

The ungainly concrete-covered yard was sliced up carefully, and the sections restacked to form short retaining walls and steps. To stick with the recycling theme, the spaces in between were filled with uncommon gravel—tumbled shards of porcelain china and mustard jars that absorb the slightest heat and keep the garden warmer than it would otherwise be.

Hardy fog-resistant grasses, bamboo and easy-to-grow calla lilies make up the verdant plant palette. Ground cover strawberries and flowering vines of black *Kennedia nigricans* are all Watts allows herself, resisting the temptation of bright flowering plants that would never do well in the sunless gloom of the neighborhood.

Color is reserved for the middle of the yard, where a pavilion of anodized aluminum framing has walls of cobalt blue and translucent white polycarbonate panels. Black plastic roses sandwiched between the panels are a nod to Victorian roses that would never thrive there. The panels, sliding on overhead tracks, are used as wind blocks when the sea breezes pick up speed.

Gardens are living sculpture and Watts likes to build piece by piece. When

she studied art in Europe she was a frequent visitor at Chaumont-sur-Loire, where experimental gardens like hers are not uncommon. Watts holds a candle to American sculptor Louise Nevelson, who used to recycle objects and box her ideas within a framework of "walls." As far as Watts is concerned, Nevelson was creating walled gardens.

In 1990, when Watts and her husband moved into a house in Alameda, she found another distraction besides art: weeding in her backyard. It was a long time before that developed into a greater understanding of how to build and plant a garden.

The Pleasures' space is her most sculptural and most interactive creation. The sliding panels change the garden's perspectives and mood each time a panel is moved. While sitting within the pavilion, the sky becomes the only constant.

THIS PAGE AND OVERLEAF: In a foggy part of San Francisco, where little grows easily, a pavilion made of aluminum framing and white and blue polycarbonate panels provides a shock of color. Plastic roses are sandwiched between panels. The gravel is made of tumbled porcelain chips.

HIDEOUT IN THE TREES
A PRINCELY GETAWAY ABOVE THE RUSSIAN RIVER NEAR HEALDSBURG

Interior designer Jeffry Weisman's Russian River property, which he inherited from the late design legend Charles Pfister, lay fallow for nearly a decade before he decided to build a summer home there with his partner, Andrew Fisher, also an interior designer and prolific artist.

They built a guesthouse and swimming pool while they toyed with the design for a main house. A wisteria thickened on its trellis by the pool, a rose garden for cut flowers thrived and formal plantings around the pool took shape. Years went by and Fisher's large *coquillage* creations—chandeliers, vases and furniture studded with seashells—forced them to expand their living and working space in their country spa setting.

So they looked to magnificent trees on the property for refuge. An extra room in a tree house was something

BELOW: At the end of the zipline, they built a mock pagoda to house a target for archery practice. RIGHT: For a spare bedroom and guest space at their weekend home in the wine country, designers Andrew Fisher and Jeffry Weisman constructed a tree house suspended from redwoods. Its detached staircase leads up to a balcony from where a zipline stretches to another end of the garden.

Fisher had dreamed of since he was a child in Michigan, climbing trees and devouring nature stories in *National Geographic* magazines. He could envision just the place.

But he discovered that making tree houses is a specialty craft. It is an arborist's task because the wrong design can kill a tree and, if a tree is not long-lived, it makes the task futile.

Fisher found Jonathan Fairbanks, a tree house expert on the Internet, who, to their dismay, dismissed their choice of a giant bay tree with views of the river as unsuitable because it would snap from the weight of a house. Fairbanks also demonstrated how the tall tree, located on a downslope, would not be so lofty after all.

A platform suspended between skinny redwoods was the way to go. An eighteen-foot-by-twenty-foot structure twenty feet off the ground, squeezed between tree branches and slender, was made tall enough to accommodate antique Indian doors the designers found in a San Francisco store. The baroque doors contrast well with the woodsy log-cabin character of the house, and their stained-glass panes please Fisher, who is also a glass artist.

This rather practical folly, accessed by an actual staircase rather than a rope ladder, is weathering well into the landscape. Inside their suspended wooden "tent," an interior as rich as tropical fruit has upholstered walls, chinoiserie, gilded accessories, a tree stump table and other allusions to trees, making it a most uncommon garden getaway.

FACING: Opulent log furniture below a twig chandelier reminds us that it is a tree house. Amid other Asian furniture, an Indian divan doubles as a bed.
ABOVE: From the tree house balcony, visitors are rewarded with views of the Russian River in the distance. The stained-glass front door is an antique from India. OVERLEAF: Inside the single-room tree house, the designers have created a living room that can be transformed into a sleeping space or art studio.

Rosehips, for medicinal herbal teas.

Bountiful Gardens

Pam Kramlich's Napa garden by Roger Warner.

SONOMA HARVEST

WORKING AMID SUNFLOWERS, FRUIT AND LAVENDER IN THE WINE COUNTRY

When interior designers Ron and Louise Mann found their rock-strewn land in Sonoma County, north of San Francisco, they were not certain how it would work. Volcanic detritus—fist-size rocks—and fine dust were not hospitable to much grass or, for that matter, the ubiquitous lavender, a Mediterranean staple, you see in wine country gardens. But more than fifteen years ago, when they started to clear their Lovall Valley crater site flanked by brown hills, live oaks and madrona, gathering rocks and relaying them as carpets of stones and stacking them as low walls, growing lavender as a crop to sell made sense.

The hot summer weather and the well-drained hills on the ten-acre farm were conducive to white, blue and purple cultivars. They brought in good soil and planted herbs in raised beds and scattered hardy sunflower seeds to naturalize.

Lavender is no longer a novelty or lucrative, but the Manns like it amid the

LEFT: A stone pear created by the Manns' gardener Geronimo, made of local lava rock, adds a sculptural accent to lavender fields at their estate in Sonoma. The lavender is sometimes used for making perfumes and body lotions. BELOW: When interior designer Ron Mann moved his atelier permanently to the country, he emptied his San Francisco warehouse of all its treasures, including old logs and lumber retrieved from riverbeds, and scattered them all around the property as landmarks.

rock and continue to irrigate and grow it. The garden's unself-conscious fields of lavender make it extraordinary.

Gradually their grange, where they fixed up ramshackle farm buildings—yet left them looking exactly as they were—became a home and not just a weekend hideout. For Ron Mann, who no longer keeps an atelier in the city, the property has become a laboratory to experiment with large stone, wood and Corten steel furniture he designs and produces. Wagon wheels, architectural fragments and steel prototypes are scattered about, awaiting their turn until the time they are needed; meanwhile, they are agricultural sculpture in the landscape. Wooden furniture and a line of hemp fabrics Mann designs are allowed to weather outdoors alongside giant logs of wood rescued from the sawmill.

In this creative setting, even their gardener Geronimo gets into the act, and in the winter he produces large fruit forms using lava rock, adobe and leftover cement, which the Manns use in interior designs.

With their own designs of walls, water features, plants and fruit, the Manns' version of Paradise would not be

LEFT: Although boulders and lava rock are never in short supply, Geronimo and the Manns have turned to pears made of painted wire as surreal garden ornaments. BELOW: In their outdoor gallery, the Manns display many ideas—stacked stone walls, stepped paths paved with local stone found on the property and Brancusi-esque sculpture designed by Mann and made in Mexico.

LEFT: Ron and Louise Mann continue to update their line of weathered, whitewashed and brightly dyed wood furniture that can be used indoors or out, shown here on a deck made of recycled roof trusses. ABOVE: Wooden *paraguas*, "umbrella" shelters the Manns designed as open-air studios for their design work, are built on simple earth-and-stone foundations, like those they've seen in Mexico. OVERLEAF: Volunteer sunflowers burst through the rock paving throughout the garden.

complete without pavilions. Since their aim to create green furniture and fabrics made of sustainable and recycled materials has led them to an indoor/outdoor aesthetic, they decided to work outdoors as much as possible. Walls would simply get in the way, they thought.

Using the same adobe, concrete and wood techniques that Geronimo builds farm structures or sculpture with, the Manns designed wooden platforms on rudimentary but sturdy hand-built adobe foundations. The wood is mainly recycled roof trusses that are laid in a herringbone pattern. Large reclaimed posts suspend a roof above each of the pavilions they call *paraguas*—Spanish for umbrella. From under these giant parasols—a version of the California bungalow sleeping porch popular at the beginning of the twentieth century—arranged close to each other, the Manns work on their designs and also commune directly with nature.

FOR A BOLD LANDSCAPE, A BOLDER GARDEN

SCULPTED LAVENDER TO COUNTER THE HYPNOTIC GEOMETRY OF NAPA

In a Napa wine country garden for video art collector Pam Kramlich, who is connected to the San Francisco Museum of Modern Art, Roger Warner has combined modernist and classical European gardening principles to spectacular effect. The rhythmic pattern of vine-covered hills needed a strong competing texture, so he installed rows of round, clipped drought-resisting lavender and a unifying massing of green shrubs, gray green tree lichens and vivid chartreuse euphorbia.

Warner has created meadows—outdoor rooms inspired by Thomas Church's Donnell garden—within highly textured planted areas. Rocks overrun with baby's tears in the middle of a meadow are performance art for a time-lapse camera to capture.

In the manner of classical European gardens, Warner also arranged trees and

BELOW: Paths lined with swaths of Nepeta take on a kinetic energy when a garden designer plants pruned balls of lavender beside them. RIGHT: Meticulously rounded lavender shrubs, planted as tightly as vines, add a powerful geometry and make a good transition from garden to vineyard.

shrubs to make the garden seem bigger. Large balls of *Teucrium fruticans* germander from North Africa that are like giant creatures in the landscape balance the visual weight of the surrounding hills and become foreground for the grander garden, which is the vineyard itself.

By blending the two areas, Warner hoped to create a garden with no dis-

cernable limit and, judging by the results, he succeeded.

Combined with rows of Fred Boutin lavender from Southern California, free-form hellebore, beds of red bark and paths lined with bluish purple nepeta, Warner's topiaries evoke some of the stately, surreal power of André Le Nôtre's classic French gardens.

PREVIOUS PAGES: Large balls of *Teucrium fruticans* from North Africa contrasted with Fred Boutin lavender shrubs are a riff on formal gardens by Le Notre. LEFT: In a shaded lawn area, Roger Warner planned sculptural compositions of rock and creeping Baby Tears. BELOW: Stone paths and steps are laid in undulating curves to contrast with the grid of the surrounding vineyards.

UNCOMMON HARVEST
SCULPTING A VEGETABLE GARDEN IN HEALDSBURG

At the end of the day, when Chalk Hill Nursery owner Kay Heafey leaves behind fields of clematis and fragrant rambling roses planted in practical, numbered rows, she retreats to a corner of the 120-acre family property, and a less ordered vegetable garden she inherited when she bought her country home.

Axial arrangements of paths and classical perspectives she has established make her country garden a kind of Versailles, but it is not too grand. There, to avoid the monotony of a commercial garden, Heafey pots citrus plants and sculpts rosemary and other topiaries. Fresh herbs, tomatoes, beans

LEFT: Here is a close-up of white florida Plena vines, one of over 300 varieties grown there.
ABOVE: The Chalk Hill clematis farm in Healdsburg, owned by Kay Heafey, first began the practice of cultivating these vines as cut flowers for the trade. Red climbing roses are mixed in among the clematis.

and lettuce overflow raised beds, and a network of gravel paths duck under redwood trellises meant for seasonal wisteria or pendulous ornamental gourds. An iron bench or café furniture at dead ends are for impromptu picnics.

In a gated meadow, Heafey has planted her favorite objects: a collection of antique English architectural fragments called staddle stones. In the dappled light under old oaks they resemble giant mushrooms that any home gardener would envy.

ABOVE: Arbors and gravel-covered walkways that lead to quiet destinations furnished with chairs and benches is one way Kay Heafey distinguishes her personal gardens around the farmhouse. Her vegetable garden, sprinkled with raised beds, potted herb topiaries and trellises for pendulous gourds is also livened by such features. RIGHT: Besides her large collection of clematis vines and her penchant for decorative vegetables, Heafey also collects antique English architectural fragments known as staddle stones. She has arranged those in a gated meadow like large mushrooms waiting for visitors, amid California live oaks and other native woods.

RIDGETOP FARMING
RESTAURATEUR PAT KULETO TENDS A YEAR-ROUND KITCHEN GARDEN

Influential restaurateur Pat Kuleto enjoys gardening but is more interested in produce for the table. The sprawling stone-and-timber house he designed on the highest ridge on his hilly, 800-acre ranch overlooking Lake Hennessy in Napa has all the extravagant, hand-crafted flair of Kuleto's many restaurant designs in the San Francisco Bay Area. A pool and flower gardens that complement it have stone terraces and places to sit and take in the sumptuous 300-degree views, but visitors are likelier to find him digging, weeding and puttering in the vegetable garden where tomatoes, asparagus, lettuce, chard and anything he wants to cook with are grown.

The quixotic, beautiful garden rises and falls in terraces around the house as if to echo the terraced vineyards of Villa Cucina that cover the surrounding hills.

It turns out there is no better way to plan a garden on such a site. Where the natural incline is left undisturbed, the

LEFT: Stands of corn and pumpkins in the light of a winter evening thrive at Villa Cucina. The garden's ridgetop location allows Kuleto to move his vegetable garden in a wide arc, in the course of the year, to catch the best sunlight. BELOW: Although growing things well is his chief goal, Kuleto, an insatiable designer, doesn't hesitate to create impromptu structures such as bamboo teepees for climbing vines. FOLLOWING PAGES: Views of Kuleto's vineyard include a glistening man-made pond, and the garden.

fractured limestone hills are battered by storms that wash away good topsoil each year. Native oaks and shrubs manage to grow there but little else survives without intervention.

There was a lot to do before the first seeds went in, but Kuleto, a one-time carpenter, enjoyed doing some of the work himself. He excavated subsoil, installed good drainage and terraced several sections with stone retaining walls. Three hundred fifty yards of fresh topsoil and mulch and great weather during the growing season made it possible to grow anything he wanted, including mature olive trees he purchased from Stags' Leap Winery for olive oil. The terraced ridgetop also allows Kuleto to get several harvests during the year because he can "follow the sun" as it shifts from season to sea-

son and grow the same things in different locations.

Some experiments led to new techniques for growing plants that might not have done so well in the windy or frosty chill of a northern California winter. Capers grow year-round only in southern Italy, but Kuleto discovered they can adapt peculiarly to frost. They die back but revive perennially, ensuring caper buds and flowers for salads and a rosehip type of fruit for pickling. Okra, first planted for his wife, who is from the south, has now become a staple you don't often see in this area.

When the growing season is good, he gets baskets brimming with sugar snap peas, edible pods and sweet peas he trains under teepees made of native reeds. In the fall, corn and pumpkin harvests ensure that no one goes hungry at Villa Cucina.

LEFT: An expressive retaining wall of soil and rock provides a well-drained site for growing herbs, lettuces and capers. BELOW: A stone driveway lined with olive and live oak trees leads to the main house. Stone wheels for crushing olives are placed like sculpture, awaiting use.

Ginkgo biloba, *used as an herbal medicine.*

Art in the Garden

Fletcher Benton's painted works from his Folded Square Alphabet series in his Napa garden.

GROUNDS FOR SCULPTURE
A GARDEN WITH WHIMSICAL YET SERIOUS DISPLAYS OF ART

Art dealer John Berggruen and his wife, Gretchen, have lived with art for as long as they can remember, but very little garden sculpture suits their small San Francisco garden. In the country, it's another story. Mid- and late-twentieth-century bronzes by several artists with a taste for whimsy, including Tom Otterness, Barry Flanagan, Nathan Oliveira and Mark diSuvero, are scattered about their eleven-acre garden and vineyard that used to belong to noted graphic designer Walter Landor.

Unlike many European and Mediterranean gardens, where statues of mythical figures and ornamental urns are placed at the ends of allées and atop pedestals, the Berggruens' abstract garden, laid out with wending paths and open stretches by Roger Warner, allows

BELOW: White oleander trained into an archway by former owner, graphics legend Walter Landor, still forms the vortexlike entry to John and Gretchen Berggruen's St. Helena home in Napa Valley.
RIGHT: The garden was originally planned by Thomas Church but altered by Roger Warner in certain areas. Near a stand of birches and flower beds, Warner clipped boxwood hedges into sculptural balls to balance the somber presence of *Bear*, a bronze statue by artist Tom Otterness.
FOLLOWING PAGES: Here is a bronze crouching frog and a view of *Bear*, both by Otterness.

for oblique views. Surprise encounters with pieces placed near a stand of birches or tucked into the shrubbery, amid flower beds and boxwood hedges clipped into giant balls, are exactly what the Berggruens want. A large, bronze hunched-over bear by Otterness broods in one corner and a rabbit by Flanagan springs up nearby. For variety, an abstract, geometric piece by Mark diSuvero is placed among the vines. The Berggruens' collection, used irreverently, looks different and comes alive in this setting where it can truly be seen in the round.

White oleander, trained by the Landors into natural archways, forms a vortexlike entrance to the estate. It is kept low—a rabbit hole—around which Warner has added fruitless mulberries. With sculpture to accent it, the garden simply has more oddball denizens to share this wonderland.

ABOVE: Among the many twentieth-century bronzes scattered discreetly around the property, the Berggruen's placed untitled painted wawa wood heads by German artist Stephan Balkenhol on colorful pedestals.
LEFT: *Boxing Hare on Anvil,* a 1989 sculpture by Bristish artist Barry Flanagan, is placed close to the house. FACING: For variation to the animal and people theme, the Berggruens placed an abstract steel work by San Francisco Bay Area artist Mark diSuvero at the edge of their vineyard.

CASA BOWES GARDEN

A PRECEDENT-SETTING MEDITERRANEAN GARDEN IN SONOMA

In Sonoma, heading north from Cornerstone Gardens, a road leads up to one of the most significant Bay Area collections of modern art—Casa Bowes, a house designed by modernist Mexican architect Ricardo Legorreta.

When owner Frances Bowes invited landscape designer Roger Warner to design a setting for sculpture around the building, naturally, given the modern castlelike stucco architecture and the terrain, he recommended a Mediterranean garden as opposed to an English-style garden Bowes has had in previous homes.

For weeks after they met, Warner discussed planting olive trees, which would never overwhelm the building—a decade before it became the tree of choice all over the wine country—until he found just the grove of gnarled, aged specimens.

He brought them in on palettes and moved them around like pieces of furniture, selecting the better ones to be close to the house. Trees have personalities,

BELOW: A planar Corten steel sculpture by Richard Serra echoes Casa Bowes' architecture.

RIGHT: The Mediterranean-style building designed by Mexican architect Ricardo Legorreta for John and Frances Bowes is complemented by a strong sculptural garden of clipped lavender by Roger Warner.

Warner insists, and he wanted to give the best of them an ideal setting. The rest were arranged behind the house, an allée that served as a wedding aisle for Bowes' daughter soon after the trees were planted.

Underplantings of rosemary, and vast lavender fields laid out in neat rows, like those Bowes and her husband, John, saw in Provence, followed on two acres surrounding the house. Dogwood, bougainvillea, wisteria, citrus trees and even a vegetable garden are all high-maintenance sections of this 400-acre former horse ranch. The lavender, for example, has to be clipped into balls regularly and replaced every few years when it gets leggy and brittle.

Warner works like an artist. With no sketches to follow, he fleshed in gardens in an organic fashion, his palette laden with lavender, chartreuse euphorbia and grasses, providing outdoor rooms off the master bedroom, around the pool and living spaces in inspired bursts. One secluded section of the garden has four magnificent oak trees, selected as canopies for a Richard Serra sculpture commissioned by the Bowes. The angular works of Donald Judd, David Smith and Richard Long are quite at home in this textural, fragrant setting.

LEFT: Amid carefully selected gnarly olive trees Roger Warner planted on the Bowes estate, a stone sculpture by Richard Long adds visual contrast. ABOVE: Warner placed some trees as sculptural objects to be viewed from inside. FOLLOWING PAGES: In another part of the garden, a surreal, beautiful allée of old olive trees and lavender has become a favored spot for family weddings.

BOLD ABSTRACT FORMS IN A CULTIVATED PARADISE
AN ARTIST'S RETREAT IS ALSO HIS OUTDOOR GALLERY

One of the last of the beatniks who has called San Francisco's North Beach area home since 1956, sculptor Fletcher Benton recalls steering the first hippies who came there looking for writer Jack Kerouac to the Haight-Ashbury, where they could find cheap rents during the tumultuous 1960s.

Decades later, with a career as a teacher at the California College of Arts and Crafts, Art Institute and San Jose University behind him, Benton contin-

ues to shape and weld the large twenty-foot-high painted or plain Corten steel compositions he became famous for.

Storing his prolific output hasn't been a problem because Benton's Napa wine country hideout atop Atlas Peak, where he thought he would work full time—but doesn't—has five acres of pine woodlands cleared of shrubs and undergrowth by an arson fire in 1981. There he can arrange his 2,000-pound pieces in clearings against a backdrop of plum and oak trees

BELOW: Fletcher Benton's rust-colored ranch-style house blends into the landscape just as his *Steel Watercolor: Cube and Ring,* a 1990 steel piece, blends in with California live oaks. RIGHT: *Rocker with Balls and X,* 2003, patinas naturally outdoors. FOLLOWING PAGES: Here is more of Benton's work, including *Donut and Balls and L,* 2002, of painted steel, standing singly, and *Straight-Up with Ball,* 2002, of oxidizing Corten steel, seen in the foreground, among a group of works.

and vineyards on neighboring hills, but far enough apart so no sculpture overlaps the other when seen in the round.

Flowers are planted sparingly, mostly around the pool close to the house, where heritage irises thrive.

When older pieces, which he used to paint, survived the fire—much to the delight of John Berggruen, whose gallery represents Benton and likes this selling point—Benton started to work with less color, allowing naturally oxidized metal to show clearly.

Concrete pads are prepared before the sculptures are hauled to the site on his crane and placed there until someone buys them. You come upon single pieces or sometimes groups from a single series hidden from immediate view, which come alive in the chiaroscuro late light that reminds Benton of a Thomas Gainsborough painting.

LEFT: The outdoor gallery—five acres of land cleared of undergrowth and trees by an arson fire—provides an unparalleled space for viewing these large works in the round. *Rocker with Balls and X,* 2003, and *Going Around the Corner,* 2002, are visible. In this sympathetic setting, Benton maintains shorn native grasses and carpets of leaves as neutral, textural counterpoints for the steel works, and low walls made of local stone are outdoor room dividers as well as places to sit on.
BELOW: Closer to the house, a slightly smaller work, *Its Harder to Do With Balls, Wave,* 1999, is of painted steel, set amid a flowering plum and native trees.

OCEAN GALLERY
SCULPTURE AS HOMAGE TO NATURE

In Bolinas, planning a garden on a small, windswept, downsloping site atop cliffs that are gradually slipping into the ocean might seem like a futile task, but that's exactly the kind of challenge for landscape architect George Hargreaves, who typically focuses on large urban projects such as devastated New Orleans or the rejuvenation of Crissy Field in San Francisco.

When he started work on this site owned by art collector Robert Bransten, whose family started MJB coffee company three generations ago, it didn't seem like much at first. Yet, considering that Hargreaves has designed only one other significant residential garden in his career (while a student at Harvard, he worked on the Minneapolis home of the Dayton family, who own Target), planning twelve acres in downtown Houston or gardens for the Stanford campus in Palo Alto began to seem a lot easier.

Bransten, who is on the acquisitions committee at the Fine Arts Museums of San Francisco, owns a collection of works by artists from the British Isles such as Damien Hirst, Richard Long and Barbara Hepworth. The blustery site was not unlike the Cornwall coast in Southern

LEFT: Robert Bransten's tiered gallery designed by landscape architect George Hargreaves allows outdoor displays of a collection of contemporary sculpture. BELOW: The simple Bolinas house now has a stepped garden with showy sculpture such as Anthony Caro's red-painted steel 1970 *Departure* near the *Echium fastuosum* and Tony Cragg's puzzling 2003 bronze, *Point of View.*

England, where Hepworth used to live, so Hargreaves decided to make the collection right at home against the view. He terraced the insignificant front yard that skirts the Branstens' cottage down toward the view. This diagonal-view corridor, gleaned from a 1940s Thomas Church design, helped to create individual platforms for each piece and also helped to silhouette the sculpture against a backdrop of sky in both directions.

By mounding the land toward the south edge of the garden, he provided raised areas to display art and quietly shield a neighbor's trailer from view.

Retaining walls of stone stacked and fitted together, stair treads and paths covered with crushed granite help to keep display areas uncluttered, but Hargreaves didn't want the rest of the garden to seem too structured. Naturally weedy areas are allowed to abut the manicured lawn in back and the precisely engineered architecture of the garden. To keep sightlines perfectly unobstructed, the only raised "wall" Hargreaves introduced here is a hedge, planted for safety, at the edge where the land falls away abruptly into sky.

But that's not all it does. It also blocks the wind, creates a sense of enclosed display space and precisely demarcates a garden landscape in the country from nature.

LEFT: The gallery of stacked-stone walls and crushed-granite beds contains, foreground to back, a 1972 bronze maquette for *Hill Arches* by Henry Moore, a 1987 aluminum pitcher, *Spill,* by Tony Cragg, a 1990 *Small Standing Circle* of slade shards by Richard Long, and Cragg's 2003 bronze, *Point of View,* which hides multiple profiles of heads within its shape. ABOVE: Surrounding a lawn that is slowly slipping into the ocean beyond, is a protective hedge of *Ceanothus* 'Julia Phelps' (small-leaf mountain lilac) and *Echium fastuosum* (Pride of Madeira). Beside it is a two-piece 1969 painted bronze sculpture by Barbara Hepworth, titled *Two Forms With White (Greek).*

Camptotheca seedpod, is used medicinally.

Exotic Collections

Bob Clark's vine-covered garden wall.

THE LEARNING GAME
BREAKING FROM GARDENING TRADITION AT HOME

Bob Clark, a garden designer known for his formal, even classical, gardens with every blade of grass in place, has broken all the rules at home. With his partner, Raul Zumba, Clark settled for a smaller house on an almost level acre of land, a former llama farm, north of Oakland where he could have a large folly—a rambling, whimsical organic garden.

He terraced the site and added walls and winding brick pathways that lead to several clearings. Flowering cherries, hundreds of roses, daturas, abutilons, potted grassy phormium and colorful *Fuchsia procumbens* make up the plant palette. Off-beat sculpture and antiques placed along paths and an experimental undulating wall studded with bottle and ceramic shards they call "Wall of China" is a good windbreak, but more importantly, it sets an irreverent mood as you enter the garden.

LEFT: Bob Clark and Raul Zumba's former llama farm is now home to a menagerie of their own, including the topiary llama that hovers over their cottage. BELOW: A lily pond is skirted by their quixotic "Wall of China," a continuous retaining wall and windbreak that contains a grouping of chartreuse-colored *Euphorbia characias wulfenii* that flowers from winter through the middle of fall.

This is Clark's laboratory, where experiments clients may not be willing to pay for or see fail can be indulged any day of the week.

Part of his strategy in creating a dense, winding garden is to prolong the experience of walking in it. Straight, linear gardens show too much too soon, and a curving line allows for a variety of plantings that don't clash with each other. In one clearing, upturned llama troughs have been recycled as benches. The resident ghost—a large llama topiary—looms above their simple cottage.

Ficus repens, a climbing vine that Clark is training using a new technique, is high maintenance, but Clark doesn't let that stop him. He prefers such gardens. Datura and over twenty other pendulous plants—also trained unnaturally—join ornamental grapefruit and orange trees. Since the garden is organic, some edible plants such as spinach can safely be planted near pesticide-free roses. That sounds practical, but Clark is pleased that picking lunch can also be a fragrant and beautiful distraction.

BELOW: Walking through the dense garden leads to surprise encounters with many ideas in Clark and Zumba's bag of tricks, including this extraordinary fence made from pruned limbs saved from clients' gardens. The path is composed of mosses, baby tears and rock pavers. RIGHT: In another section of the garden, a different kind of walkway, tidily paved with brick, has a rich weave of plants, grasses, colors and textures bordering it, including pendulous yellow *Datura arborea,* several types of carex and *Phormium tenax* 'Purpureum', also known as purple New Zealand flax.

GALLERY GARDEN
PLANTS, SCULPTURE AND MYTH VIE FOR ATTENTION IN BERKELEY

Sculptor Marcia Donahue's small Berkeley garden is a riot of textures and forms. It is a sculpture garden, but it is so densely planted you have to go hunting for a rotating show of art and esoteric objects hidden among grasses, shrubs and lilies along a figure-eight pathway of brick and stone. It is also a backdrop for her permanent collection of Mark Bullwinkle rusted-steel animals and birds of paradise in the branches of fruit trees, and large Easter Island–esque head sculptures she carves from stone.

Mythic rituals and visual puns amuse Donahue, who combines her ceramic and plaster totems with Daphne and Flora, figures from Greek and Roman mythology, alongside Adam and Eve. A blue bottle tree, a tradition among black families in the South, is combined with

LEFT: Marcia Donahue's "Our Own Stuff Gallery Garden" is a laboratory of propogated plants and grasses, especially blue bamboo, and it is liberally planted with her own ceramic and stone sculpture and works by fellow artists such as Mark Bullwinkle. Here, reddish ceramic bamboo that she sells commercially, titled "Bambusa Ceramica Sancta" competes with the real thing. BELOW: This is a view of the front porch to her painted Victorian home and office, where salvaged glass lamp shades are strung together in a totem. Eyes, painted in the Egyptian style, watch all visitors. FOLLOWING PAGES: A stone head and bamboo sculpture by Donahue amid *Gunnera tinctoria.*

cypresses pruned to look like spiraling corkscrews. The Corten steel garden gate she commissioned from Bullwinkle is in the shape of two hands—her favorite garden tools—and gravestones cover the compost heap.

Donahue, a self-taught gardener, is also one of the Hortisexualist plant propagators and is fascinated by the variety she can have in the East Bay's clement weather.

Colorful bamboo, a giant grass from the foothills of the Himalayas, Mexico and Japan, grows easily over twenty feet high but is not too daunting for this city gardener.

Bamboo, clumped in tall blue or pink clusters or "running" (where the roots spread to form new shoots), can be trimmed low as ground cover. It needs little water and likes slopes, and so Donahue, who opens her Our Own Stuff Garden Gallery to visitors on Sundays, has collected over thirty colorful bamboo varieties in her quest for an even more artful, gaudy gallery.

LEFT: Mark Bullwinkle's Corten steel pieces and Maria Donahue's bamboo amid potted succulents. BELOW: Donahue's blue bottle tree and corkscrew topiaries are near a figure of Flora seated on a white pedestal.

MAYBECK'S HIDEAWAY
AN ENDURING HILLSIDE GARDEN FOR A HISTORIC BERKELEY COTTAGE

Horticulturist Roger Raiche, a museum scientist, used to work at the UC Botanical Gardens. Now at his own firm—Planet Horticulture near Calistoga—he is a dilettante architect as well, in part because of the Berkeley garden he used to share with his partner, David McRory.

After a great fire in the 1930s, their small house was built by none other than architect Bernard Maybeck, who tried to make it fire resistant by molding some concrete walls in cement sacks. Raiche and McRory designed an equally enduring hillside garden for it—one the home's new owners preserve. They built walls, paths, terraces and mounds to break up the steep hillside garden into magical grottos and seating areas. Because the

LEFT: Here, Raiche and McRory's richly textured garden, with grasses and succulents mixed for form and color, contains a quiet clearing of lawn punctuated with stepping-stones.

ABOVE: Roger Raiche and David McRory's historic cottage, that architect Bernard Maybeck built after a San Francisco Bay Area fire engulfed the Berkeley hills in the 1930s, has a didactic garden with many lessons about safety, plants and garden structure. The house has some cement walls that Maybeck molded in sacks (not shown), and only a few plants are allowed close to the structure.

garden is steeply terraced, over a thousand different species of plants, arranged like trees in larger estate gardens, can be viewed silhouetted up against the sky.

Unusual flowering plants and ornamentals (Raiche and McRory belong to a group of experimental gardeners known as the Hortisexualists, who propagate hybrids and rare plant species) are contrasted with phormiums (New Zealand flax), cussonias (an African cabbage tree), and a variety of pelargoniums, sedges and other ornamental grasses.

Texture and color in small areas are contrasted with expanses of green grass. The textures may seem random but are so carefully planned that the same path from one space to the next seems different when you turn back.

Such freehand compositions are scene changes where Raiche directs plants, but they are not his principal actors. In Raiche and McRory's world, urns, cement pipes and rusty objects are as important as plants. Their balancing act between animate and inanimate is not intended to be cutting edge, but it has to be simply beautiful.

THIS PAGE AND FACING: Large urns form a kind of architecture around which to build a garden according to Roger Raiche and David McRory, who run their firm, Planet Horticulture, from offices in Calistoga and San Francisco. Paths laid with different materials and in different patterns make even a small garden seem larger. Beds, and in fact the entire garden too, are planted in tiers so that low as well as tall palms and pendulous plants are clearly visible. The designers also like to secrete whimsical objects within low grasses.

HILLTOP WONDERLAND
SUCCULENTS, GRASSES AND AN OLD OAK TREE NEAR MOUNT TAMALPAIS

Although Elena Mills Mandin's three-acre hillside property in Kentfield, Marin County, was hot and dry in the summer, buffeted by winds and regularly devastated by marauding deer, garden designer Brandon Tyson wasn't discouraged.

Few gardeners could have resisted the view of Mount Tamalpais, a peak sacred to the Indians, and an ancient oak close to Mandin's house. The flat ranch home that existed there had lawns and low plantings, but the flattened garden desperately needed some contours. To get a sense of intimacy and discovery in that open space, Tyson decided to create undulating "rooms," each with distinctive plants from South Africa, Japan and tropical countries.

In this private botanical park, a path of river wash stones cuts across a shag carpet of *Ophiopogon japonicus* (mondo grass) planted in swirling mounds. Bare smooth-limbed Japanese maples rise

LEFT: Tamalpais mountain overlooks Elena Mills Mandin's Kentfield garden, where designer Brandon Tyson has collected succulents, ornamental grasses, lacy *Aralia*, 'Century Plant' agave, and spindly *Washingtonia robusta* palms. BELOW: A potted *Brahea armata* sits near the pool, which is close to a century-old oak tree kept free of underplantings that can lead to overwatering.

above the kinetic grass. Next to the swimming pool, *Butia capitata* (pindo palm) and *Carex stricta* 'Bowles Golden' sedge add texture.

In another section, the spiky glossy leaves of *Araucaria araucana* (monkey puzzle trees) contrast with *Trachycarpus fortunei* (Chinese windmill palm). Mixed in, many hard-to-find South African bulbs and ornamental grasses from New Zealand naturalized easily in the Bay Area's climate. Their colors, foliage and texture, Tyson thought, would look better than tidy tulips.

Deer are kept away from lime-green *Luzula sylvatica* 'Aurea' and deep burgundy grasses with concealed fencing. *Heuchera* 'Plum Pudding', or *Pyrrosia lingua* 'Cristata', are safely under the oak, since it is perched on a slope where irrigation won't rot its roots. Japanese maples and bulbs throw color into the mix every spring, and in the summer the garden is at its peak when Mediterranean plants in Tyson's palette sprout, seed and spread.

Tyson's adage—"Big places need big plants"—was also true here. A rare collection of large agaves, including *Agave americana* 'Mediopicta', and *Agave victoriae-reginae*, a stand of endangered monkey puzzle trees native to Chile, and many kinds of palms create a sculptural but unfussy foreground.

Even though these plants don't look large against the mountain, they were so big that they had to be craned in. *Brahea armata* (Mexican blue palm), *Butia capitata* (pindo palm), *Phoenix canariensis* (Canary Island date palm), *Cycas revoluta* (sago palm) or *Trachycarpus fortunei* (Chinese windmill palm) fare well even though in the frequent winds and rain they flail about like shamans.

It's a new world for Mandin. But even in the most remote sections of her exotic garden, a rain-fed mountain that seems green year-round, heirloom palms and an old oak tree all anchor her view.

ABOVE: A carpet of *Ophiopogon japonicus* (mondo) grass planted in mounds is an animated foil to the sleek bare limbs of Japanese maples and river wash stone pavers. LEFT: A spiky *Dasylirion longissimum* (Sotol) grows above clumps of euphorbia, aloes and *Agave victoriae-reginae* tucked in among river rocks. RIGHT: Spiky glossy-leaved *Araucaria araucana* (monkey puzzle trees) look like fake Christmas trees. *Trachycarpus fortunei* (Chinese windmill palm), a Brandon Tyson favorite, adds strong vertical lines to the garden.

Catharanthus roseus, used in traditional herbal medicine

Healing Gardens

The Labyrinth at Grace Cathedral in San Francisco.

A MOUNTAIN OF HISTORIC STONE BECOMES A JAPANESE GARDEN

Cevan Forristt, a San Jose garden designer with a nose for exotic Eastern artifacts and statuary for gardens, landed a haul of granite from a demolished seminary building next to Grace Cathedral in San Francisco. The seminary, it turned out, had been built on the site of the Crocker mansion destroyed in the 1906 earthquake, and much of its stone had been salvaged from the ruins. The stone was blocky and uninteresting, and this time no one but Forristt would take it.

As luck would have it, just about the time Forristt hauled tons of it away,

Molly and Steve Westrate, who had lived in Japan, asked him to build them a garden that resembled a historic Kyoto garden on their sheltered one-acre property in Woodside.

Forristt's signature pastiche of many Southeast Asian styles—lily ponds, bamboo fountains and statuary arranged in garden shrines—is always calming, but here was his chance to fashion an all-Japanese-style garden and he couldn't resist.

The Westrates' bare hillside backdrop, flat manicured lawns and prosaic

ABOVE: A Japanese-style torii gate designed by Cevan Forristt for a Woodside garden has such heavy timbers that its parts needed to be craned in. Hand-picked salvaged granite blocks from buildings around Grace Cathedral in San Francisco were used for steps and an entry path.

RIGHT: In the garden, more stone is used for straight and curving walls and steps up the hillside.

plantings fenced in with jasmine-covered chain-link were altered or quickly removed.

The smallest stones were piled to form mounds over level sections, and more rubble was allowed to cascade down the hillside amid new bamboo groves.

Larger corbel arches and paving stones mixed within his stone inventory made the rest of Forristt's task one of slow excavation.

The largest pieces—forty-inch-square blocks—were easily transformed into birdbaths or fountains, and to match the scale of many of those stones, twelve-by-twelve-inch redwood posts were used to make a massive torii gateway. Large, flat stones were used as steps at the entry gate, and smaller ones became paving for a path to the front door of the Westrates' modernist Rudolph & Sletten house.

With one helper and a backhoe, Forristt selected and laid stones as carefully as if he were creating a fine mosaic, moving large and small stones with equal care. The walkway from the front gate to the back of the garden alone took several days to arrange because shaping walls, pathways and stairways simultaneously was simply a matter of choosing the right stone rather than following any master plan or strict Japanese iconography.

Although it is Japanese at first glance, this garden does not feel as still or prescribed as a Zen garden might have been. Instead, it is infused with a rambling English spirit replete with seasonal shows of pomegranate, persimmon and flowering quince, and grassy beds and stone paths that bob and weave from view.

LEFT: A ceramic elephant greets visitors walking up the path made of salvaged granite. In the foreground, the wall ends in a chunk of square granite, hollowed into a basin. ABOVE: The torii gate, viewed from inside, is draped with flowering vines and is flanked on the left by a birdhouse.

FOLLOWING ZEN
A JAPANESE INSTALLATION AMID APPLE ORCHARDS

Thirty hilly acres of apple orchards, redwood forest and a few open meadows in Sebastopol, within an hour of San Francisco, were just right for arts patron Ann Hatch, who has, over several decades, built a compound filled with art on her land. Hatch's family established the Walker Art Center in Minneapolis, and her own compound is intended to be an eclectic gathering spot for artists and friends.

In this part of Sonoma County, vineyards had been eradicated during prohibition, and Hatch's orchards of Gravenstein, Jonathan, Rome and Golden Delicious apples are a legacy of the era. The home on three acres at the orchard's edge, designed by her husband, Paul Discoe, who is an ordained Buddhist priest trained in Japanese temple joinery, has a distinctly Japanese architecture.

To make things more cohesive, Discoe suggested a garden to match, and Ron Herman, who trained in classical Japanese garden culture and who frequently teaches in Kyoto as well as Berkeley, has designed a landscape complement.

LEFT AND BELOW: Lavender is a fragrant swath of color planted between rows of apple trees in Ann Hatch's Sebastopol orchard, where Hatch's husband, Paul Discoe, of Joinery Structures, has built a Japanese temple-style weekend home. Around it, Ron Herman, who collaborated with Discoe on a Japanese-style estate for Larry Ellison, has designed a Zen garden.

Both architect and landscape designer have also collaborated on an ambitious Japanese-style estate in Woodside for Oracle's Larry Ellison. But unlike Ellison, Hatch viewed her home and garden as separate art installations, punctuated by eclectic sculpture scattered in the orchard.

A fence of woven wooden slats surrounds the garden, which has a swimming pool and water garden in the center, arranged to align with the rows of apple trees interspersed with swaths of French lavender close to the house.

Hand-cast concrete pavers abut the pool, and the more free-form beds and paths surrounding these are a collaborative installation between Herman and Discoe.

As a crowning feature, Herman invited Shigeru Namba, a classically trained Japanese rock master to arrange seventy-five tons of boulders within Hatch's sanctuary, which, with its blend of orchards, painterly lavender and stylized outcroppings in the manner of Zen settings in Kyoto, is a multicultural installation and a symbol of the Western melting pot.

LEFT: Boulders trucked onto the site were carefully arranged to simulate natural outcroppings of rock. Stepped retaining walls provide seating poolside. The large square pavers around the pool are individually hand-cast concrete. ABOVE: A handmade woven wood fence by Paul Discoe, an ordained Buddhist priest who learned the art of temple building in Japan, surrounds the compound.

GARDENING WITH REVERENCE
CEVAN FORRISTT FINDS TEXTURAL AND SPIRITUAL BALANCE IN THE GARDEN

In a corner of San Jose, garden designer Cevan Forristt has transformed his quarter-acre home and garden as a retreat to evoke places he's been to in Java, Myanmar and India.

The first time he heard gamelan music in San Jose, he was inexorably drawn to Asia. He discovered a facsimile of Asia in Golden Gate Park at the Japanese Tea Gardens, but it wasn't until he saw the real thing that he fully comprehended its spiritual draw.

In his home, statues of Buddha and Hindu gods are arranged with a sense of reverence—on high planes or a pedestal—in rooms dressed with gilded murals reminiscent of those in Southeast Asia. Granite and bronze objects and wall paintings rendered with fingers and palms set the mood. Open rooms—pavilions for worship, where birds flit in and out easily—flow one into the other. And because gardening has become Forristt's solitary art out of necessity, marigolds

BELOW: At home in San Jose, garden designer Cevan Forristt has created a setting like those he visits while shopping in Asia for garden objects. A gate he designed is fitted with handles from Thailand. RIGHT: Architectural stone fragments from Asia and the United States suggest ancient ruins around a koi pond. FOLLOWING PAGES: Here are temples inside Forristt's home.

from his garden, arranged in *mandala* patterns, are offered to the gods as thanks for their company.

Growing flowers for such use becomes a form of meditation for this gardener, and Forristt's textural, tropical excesses spill into the garden. In this baroque version of his dream continent, shallow pools of water, fountains, stone walkways, and lacy plants to shade the koi abound. His garden is an eastern temple compound with western amenities. Add old Vietnamese doors, gongs, architectural fragments and gaudy, gilded Thai furniture made to look like Chinese originals and you get Forristt's giddy pastiche.

An avid horticulturist and a member of the Bay Area's Hortisexualists, who grouped together to visit private gardens and propagate exotic plant species, Forristt has his creations, banana palms and lilies, growing in the heart of an evolving blue-collar district. This delicious juxtaposition makes his fake temple ruin—like the Rosicrucian Egyptian temple nearby—feel both ancient and futuristic all at once.

LEFT: Warehouse and muse, Forristt's home is an endless source of inspiration for clients' projects, but it is also where he goes to relax amid Buddha figures and statues of Hindu gods hidden among the ferns. BELOW: Ponds are essential features in many of his gardens, as they are at his home, but Forristt also finds the sound of flowing water healing. This water fountain was created by casually stacking some of the architectural stone fragments and basins he has in his collection.

Aconitum napellus, *used in Ayurvedic medicine.*

Echinacea, *an herbal plant used in Chinese medicine.*

Resources

GARDEN DESIGNERS

Alma Hecht
Second Nature Design
San Francisco, CA 94112
(415) 586-6578
www.secondnature.bz
Sustainable landscapes.

Andrea Cochran
Andrea Cochran Landscape
Architecture
2325 Third Street, #210
San Francisco, CA 94107
(415) 503-0060
www.acochran.com

Andrew Fisher and Jeffry Weisman
Fisher Weisman Design & Decoration
616 Minna Street
San Francisco, CA 94103
(415) 255-2254
www.fisherweisman.com

Andy Cao
Cao|Perrot Studio
3511 West 6th Street, Studio 5
Los Angeles, CA 90020
(213) 458-2900
www.caoperrotstudio.com

Bernard Trainor
Bernard Trainor + Associates
171 Central Avenue
Pacific Grove, CA 93950
(831) 655-1414
www.bernardtrainor.com

Bob Clark
Bob Clark Designs
11205 Ettrick Street
Oakland, CA 94605
(510) 633-1391

Brandon Tyson
1910 Old Sonoma Road
Napa, CA 94559
(707) 257-0985

Cevan Forristt
P.O. Box 1567
San Jose, CA 95109
(408) 297-8538
www.forristt.com

David McRory and Roger Raiche
Planet Horticulture
3487 Old Lawley Toll Road
Calistoga, CA 94515
(707) 942-0499
(415) 827-4342
(800) 572-7922
www.planethorticulture.com

David Weingarten
Ace Architects
330 Second Street, No. 1
Oakland, CA 94607
(510) 452-0775
www.aceland.com

Eric and Silvina Blasen
Blasen Landscape Architecture
2344 Marinship Way
Sausalito, CA 94965
(415) 332-5329
www.blasengardens.com

Fletcher Benton
Fletcher Benton Studio
250 Dore Street
San Francisco, CA 94103
(415) 863-7207
www.fletcherbenton.com

George Hargreaves
Hargreaves Associates
398 Kansas Street
San Francisco, CA 94103
(415) 865-1811
www.hargreaves.com

Jack Chandler
Chandler and Chandler
68 Coombs Street, Suite L-5
Napa, CA 94559
(707) 253-8266
www.chandler2.com

Joseph Marek
Joseph Marek Landscape Architecture
2252 - 25th Street
Santa Monica, CA 90405
(310) 399-7923
www.josephmarek.com

Kay Heafey
Chalk Hill Clematis
P.O. Box 1847
Healdsburg, CA 95448
(707) 433-8416
www.chalkhillclematis.com

Marcia Donahue
Our Own Stuff Gallery-Garden
3017 Wheeler Street
Berkeley, CA 94705
(510) 540-8544

Nancy Goslee Power
Nancy Goslee Power & Associates
1660 Stanford Street
Santa Monica, CA 90404
(310) 264-0266
www.nancypower.com

Olle Lundberg
Lundberg Design
2620 Third Street
San Francisco, CA 94107
(415) 695-0110
www.lundbergdesign.com

Pamela Burton & Company
1430 Olympic Boulevard
Santa Monica, CA 90404
(310) 828-6373
www.pamelaburtonco.com

Pat Kuleto
55 Francisco Street, Suite 430
San Francisco, CA 94133
(415) 474-9669
www.kuleto.com

Rebecca Sams and Buell Steelman
Mosaic Garden Design & Construction
P.O. Box 50623
Eugene, OR 97405
(541) 434-6467
www.mosaic-gardens.com

Roger Warner
Roger Warner Garden Design
P.O. Box 331
Saint Helena, CA 94574
(707) 963-1950
www.rogerwarnergardendesign.com

Ron and Louise Mann
P.O. Box 204
Vineburg, CA 95487
(707) 935-3991
(415) 994-9798
www.ronmanndesign.com

Ron Herman
Ron Herman Landscape Architect
261 Joaquin Avenue
San Leandro, CA 94577
(510) 352-4920
www.rherman.com

Ron Lutsko
Lutsko Associates Landscape
2815 - 18th Street
San Francisco, CA 94110
(415) 920-2800
www.lutskoassociates.com

Shirley Alexandra Watts
Sawattsdesign: landscape
and installation
1000 Park Street
Alameda, CA 94501
(510) 521-5223
www.sawattsdesign.com

Thomas and Cindy Krumholz
13155 McNally Road
Valley Center, CA 92082
(760) 739-0462

Tina Beebe
Moore Ruble Yudell Architects &
Planners
933 Pico Boulevard
Santa Monica, CA 90405
(310) 450-1400
www.moorerubleyudell.com

Topher Delaney
T. Delaney/SEAM STUDIO
600 Illinois Street
San Francisco, CA 94107
(415) 621-9899
tdelaney.com
tdelaney@tdelaney.com

Walter Hood
Hood Design
3016 Filbert Street, Ste. #2
Oakland, CA 94608
(510) 595-0688
www.wjhooddesign.com

GARDEN NURSERIES

Albion Ridge Nursery
30901 Albion Ridge Road
Albion, CA 95410
(707) 937-1835
www.albionridgenursery.com

Alden Lane Nursery
981 Alden Lane
Livermore, CA 94550
(925) 447-0280
www.aldenlane.com

Alrie Middlebrook
Middlebrook Gardens
76 Race Street
San Jose, CA 95126
(408) 292-9993
www.middlebrook-gardens.com

Al's Nursery
900 Portola Road
Portola Valley, CA 94028
(650) 851-0206

Annie's Annuals
740 Market Street
Richmond, CA 94801
(510) 215-1326
www.anniesannuals.com

Antonelli Brothers Begonia Gardens
2545 Capitola Road
Santa Cruz, CA 95062
(831) 475-5222
By appointment only
www.antonellibegonias.com

Bassignani Nursery
1841 Gravenstein Highway S.
Sebastopol, CA 95472
(707) 823-3984

Bay Natives
An online nursery
www.baynatives.com

Benicia Garden & Nursery
126 East E Street
Benicia, CA 94510
(707) 747-9094
www.beniciagarden.com

Berkeley Horticultural Nursery
1310 McGee Avenue
Berkeley, CA 94703
(510) 526-4704
www.berkeleyhort.com

Big River Nurseries
44850 Comptche Ukiah Road
Mendocino, CA 95460
(707) 937-5026

Boething Treeland Farms
2923 Alpine Road
Portola Valley, CA 94028
(650) 851-4770
(800) 272-8733
www.boethingtreeland.com

Bongard's Treescape Nursery
12460 San Mateo Road
Half Moon Bay, CA 94019
(650) 726-4568

Broadmoor Lumber & Landscape Supply
1350 El Camino Real
South San Francisco, CA 95080
(650) 761-1515
www.broadmoorlumber.com

Cactus Jungle
1509 - 4th Street
Berkeley, CA 94710
(510) 558-8650
www.cactusjungle.com

California Carnivores
2833 Old Gravenstein Highway S.
Sebastopol, CA 95472
(707) 824-0433
Insect-eating plants
www.californiacarnivores.com

California Flora Nursery
2990 Somers Street
Fulton, CA 95439
(707) 528-8813
www.calfloranursery.com

Chalk Hill Clematis Nursery
P.O. Box 1847
Healdsburg, CA 95448
(707) 433-8416
www.chalkhillclematis.com

Cistus Nursery
22711 NW Gillihan Road
Sauvie Island, OR 94231
(503) 621-2233
www.cistus.com

Common Ground Organic Garden Supply and Education Center
559 College Avenue
Palo Alto, CA 94306
(650) 493-6072
www.commongroundinpaloalto.org

Cornflower Farms
9811 Sheldon Road
Elk Grove, CA 95624
(916) 689-1015
www.cornflowerfarms.com
By appointment, wholesale native plants.

Cottage Garden Growers
3995 Emerald Drive
Petaluma, CA 94952
(707) 778-8025
www.cottagegardensofpet.com

Cottage Gardens of Bennett Valley
2780 Yulupa Avenue
Santa Rosa, CA 95405
(707) 569-8624

Cypress Flower Farm
333 Cypress Avenue
Moss Beach, CA 94038
(650) 728-0728
www.cypressflowerfarm.com

Desert Botanical Garden
1201 North Galvin Parkway
Phoenix, AZ 85008
(480) 941-1225
www.dbg.org

Digging Dog Nursery
P.O. Box 471
Albion, CA 95410
(707) 937-1130
www.diggingdog.com
A mail-order nursery.

East Bay Nursery
2332 San Pablo Avenue
Berkeley, CA 94702
(510) 845-6490
www.eastbaynursery.com

Elkhorn Native Plant Nursery
1957B Highway 1
Moss Landing, CA 95039
(831) 763-1207
www.elkhornnursery.com

Emerisa Gardens
555 Irwin Lane
Santa Rosa, CA 95401
(707) 525-9600

Flora Grubb Gardens
1634 Jerrold Avenue
San Francisco, CA 94124
(415) 626-7256
www.floragrubb.com

Garden Valley Ranch Rose Nursery
498 Pepper Road
Petaluma, CA 94952
(707) 795-0919
www.gardenvalley.com

Golden Nursery
1122 - 2nd Avenue
San Mateo, CA 94401
(650) 348-5525
www.goldennursery.com

Great Petaluma Desert
5010 Bodega Avenue
Petaluma, CA 94952
(707) 778-8278
www.gpdesert.com

Healdsburg Nursery
12950 Old Redwood Highway
Healdsburg, CA 95448
(707) 433-8904
www.healdsburg-nursery.com

Landscape Unlimited
4330 Bodega Avenue
Petaluma, CA 94952
(707) 778-0136

Las Baulines Nursery
150 Olema Bolinas Road
Bolinas, CA 94924
(415) 868-0808

Lyngso Garden Materials
19 Seaport Boulevard
Redwood City, CA 94063
(650) 364-1730
www.lyngsogarden.com

Magic Gardens
729 Heinz Avenue
Berkeley, CA 94710
(510) 644-2351
www.magicgardens.com

Mendocino Maples Nursery
41569 Little Lake Road
Mendocino, CA 95460
(707) 937-1189
www.mendocinomaples.com

Miniature Plant Kingdom
13404 Harrison Grade Place
Sebastopol, CA 95472
(707) 874-2233
www.miniplantkingdom.com

Mostly Natives Nursery
P.O. Box 258
27235 Highway One
Tomales, CA 94971
(707) 878-2009
www.mostlynatives.com

Native Revival Nursery
2600 Mar Vista Drive
Aptos, CA 95003
(831) 684-1811
www.nativerevival.com

Native Sons Nursery
379 West El Campo
Arroyo Grande, CA 93420
(805) 481-5996

Navlet's Garden Center
46100 Warm Springs Boulevard
Fremont, CA 94539
(510) 657-7511
www.navletsgardens.com

Neon Palm Nursery
3525 Stony Point Road
Santa Rosa, CA 95407
(707) 585-8100

North Coast Native Nursery
P.O. Box 660
Petaluma, CA 94953
(707) 769-1213
www.northcoastnativenursery.com

Ogawa-Mune Nursery
123 Mayhews Road
Fremont, CA 94536
(510) 793-7123
www.ogawamune.com

Passanisi Nursery, Inc.
8270 Petaluma Hill Road
Penngrove, CA 94951
(707) 792-2674
www.passanisinursery.com

Peacock Horticultural Nursery
4296 Gravenstein Highway S.
Sebastopol, CA 95472
(707) 291-0547

Pond & Garden
6225 Stony Point Road
Cotati, CA 94931
(707) 792-9141

Ragen & Associates
517 East Pike Street
Seattle, WA 98122
(206) 329-4737
www.ragenassociates.com

Rana Creek Wholesale Nursery
35351 East Carmel Valley Road
Carmel Valley, CA 93924
(831) 659-2830
www.ranacreeknursery.com

Regan's Nursery
4268 Decoto Road
Fremont, CA 94555
(510) 797-3222

Roger Reynolds Nursery
& Carriage Stop
133 Encinal Avenue
Menlo Park, CA 94025
(650) 323-5612
www.rogerreynoldsnursery.com

San Miguel Greenhouses
936 San Miguel Road
Concord, CA 94518
(925) 798-0476

Sloat Garden Center
2700 Sloat Boulevard
San Francisco, CA 94116
(415) 566-4415
www.sloatgardens.com

Sonoma Horticultural Nursery
3970 Azalea Avenue
Sebastopol, CA 95472
(707) 823-6832
www.sonomahort.com

Stanley & Sons Nursery
11740 SE Orient Drive
Boring, OR 97009
(503) 663-4391
www.stanleyandsons.com

Sumigawa Nursery
8049 Gravenstein Highway
Cotati, CA 94931
(707) 795-5467

Sunnyside Nursery
130 Sir Francis Drake Boulevard
San Anselmo, CA 94960
(415) 453-2701
www.sunnysideofmarin.com

Tassajara Nursery
2550 Camino Tassajara
Danville, CA 94506
(925) 736-7600

The Dry Garden Nursery
6556 Shattuck Avenue
Oakland, CA 94609
(510) 547-3564

The Urban Farmer Store
653 East Blithedale
Mill Valley, CA 94941
(415) 380-3840
www.urbanfarmerstore.com

Thomsen's Garden Center
1113 Lincoln Avenue
Alameda, CA 94501
(510) 522-3265

Thornhill Nursery
6250 Thornhill Drive
Oakland, CA 94611
(510) 339-1311

Tyler's Carlmont Nursery
2029 Ralston Avenue
Belmont, CA 94002
(650) 591-6845

Valley Oak Nursery
7021 Lone Tree Way
Brentwood, CA 94513
(925) 516-7868
www.valleyoaknursery.com

Vintage Gardens
4130 Gravenstein Highway N.
Sebastopol, CA 95472
(707) 829-2035
www.vintagegardens.com

West End Nursery
1938 - 5th Avenue
San Rafael, CA 94901
(415) 454-4175

Western Garden Nursery
2756 Vineyard Avenue
Pleasanton, CA 94566
(925) 462-1760
www.westerngardennursery.com

Western Hills Nursery
16250 Coleman Valley Road
Occidental, CA 95465
(707) 874-3731
www.westernhillsnursery.com

Whiting Nursery
738 Main Street
St. Helena, CA 94574
(707) 963-5358
www.whitings.com

Wild Bird Center
926 El Camino Real
San Carlos, CA 94070
(650) 595-0300
www.wildbirdcenter.com

Yabusaki's Dwight Way Nursery
1001 Dwight Way
Berkeley, CA 94710
(510) 845-6261

Yerba Buena Nursery
19500 Skyline Boulevard
Woodside, CA 94062
(415) 851-1668
www.yerbabuenanursery.com

OPEN GARDENS

American Public Gardens Association
www.aabga.org

Cornerstone Festival of Gardens
23570 Highway 121
Sonoma, CA 95476
(707) 933-3010
www.cornerstonegardens.com

Mendocino Coast Botanical Gardens
18220 North Highway 1
Fort Bragg, CA 95437
(707) 964-4352
www.gardenbythesea.org

National Tropical Botanical Garden
Southshore Visitors Center
4425 Lawai Road
Poipu, Kauai, HI 96756
(808) 742-2623
www.ntbg.org

Rancho Santa Ana Botanic Garden
1500 North College Avenue
Claremont, CA 91711
(909) 625-8767
www.rsabg.org

Red Butte Garden
300 Wakara Way
Salt Lake City, UT 84108
(801) 581-4747
www.redbuttegarden.org

San Francisco Botanical Garden at Strybing
Arboretum
Ninth Ave., at Lincoln Way
San Francisco, CA 94122
(415) 661-1316
www.sfbotanicalgarden.org

Sigmund Stern Grove
(415) 252-6252
www.sterngrove.org

The Huntington Botanical Gardens
1151 Oxford Road
San Marino, CA 91108
(626) 405-2100
www.huntingtonbotanical.org

The Living Desert
47-900 Portola Avenue
Palm Desert, CA 92260
(760) 346-5694

The Ruth Bancroft Garden
1500 Bancroft Road
Walnut Creek, CA 94598
(925) 210-9663
www.ruthbancroftgarden.org

U.C. Davis Arboretum
1 Shields Avenue
Davis, CA 95616
(530) 752-4880
www.arboretum.ucdavis.edu

University of California Botanical Garden
200 Centennial Drive
Berkeley, CA 94720
(510) 643-2755

University of Washington Botanic Gardens
2300 Arboretum Drive East
Seattle, WA 98105
(206) 543-8800
www.uwbotanicgardens.org

STORES / WEB SITES

Artefact Design and Salvage
23562 Highway 121
Sonoma, CA 95476
(707) 933-0660
www.artefactdesignsalvage.com

Big Red Sun
1102 E Cesar Chavez Street
Austin, TX 78702
(512) 480-9749
www.bigredsun.com

Concreteworks
1137 – 57th Avenue
Oakland, CA 94621
(510) 534-7141
www.concreteworks.com

Flora Grubb Gardens
1634 Jerrold Avenue
San Francisco, CA 94124
(415) 626-7256
www.floragrubb.com

Gardens
1818 West 35th Street
Austin, TX 78703
(512) 451-5490
www.gardens-austin.com

GRDN: For the Urban Gardener
103 Hoyt Street
Brooklyn, NY 11217
(718) 797-3628
www.grdnbklyn.com

Inner Gardens: Art for the Garden
6050 West Jefferson Boulevard
Los Angeles, CA 90016
(310) 838-8378
www.innergardens.com

Limn Collection
290 Townsend Street
San Francisco, CA 94107
(415) 977-1300
www.limn.com
Outdoor furniture.

Living Green Plantscape Design
150C - 15th Street
San Francisco, CA 94103
(415) 864-2251
www.livinggreen.com

Paxton Gate
824 Valencia Street
San Francisco, CA 94110
(415) 824-1872
www.paxtongate.com

Plant It Earth
2279 Market Street
San Francisco, CA 94114
(415) 626-5082
www.plantitearth.com

Sierra Azul
2660 East Lake Avenue
Watsonville, CA 95076
(831) 763-0939
www.sierraazul.com

The Gardener
1836 Fourth Street
Berkeley, CA 94710
(510) 548-4545
or
520 Dry Creek Road
Healdsburg, CA 95448
(707) 431-1063
or
One Ferry Building
San Francisco, CA 94111
(415) 981-8181
www.thegardener.com

The Magazine
1823 Eastshore Highway
Berkeley, CA 94710
(510) 549-2282
www.themagazine.info
Outdoor furniture.

Wheeler Zamaroni
3500 Petaluma Hill Road
Santa Rosa, CA 95404
(707) 543-8400
www.wzsupply.com

Zinc Details
1905 Fillmore Street
San Francisco, CA 94115
(415) 776-2100
Outdoor furniture.
or
2410 California Street
San Francisco, CA 94115
(415) 776-9002
www.zincdetails.com

BIBLIOGRAPHY

Appleton, Marc. *California Mediterranean.* New York:
Rizzoli, 2007.

Bay, De, and James Bolton. *Garden Mania.* New York:
Clarkson Potter, 2000.

Bosser, Jacques. *Gardens in Time.* New York: Harry N.
Abrams, 2006.

Brawley Hill, May. *On Foreign Soil (American Gardeners
Abroad).* New York: Harry N. Abrams, 2005.

Browning, Dominique, and the editors of *House & Garden.
The New Garden Paradise (Great Private Gardens of the
World).* New York: W. W. Norton, 2005.

Fryberger, Betsy G., ed. *The Changing Garden (Four
Centuries of European and American Art).* Berkeley:
University of California Press, 2003.

Hobhouse, Penelope. *In Search of Paradise (Great Gardens
of the World).* London: Frances Lincoln Limited, 2006.

Silva, Roberto. *New Brazilian Gardens: The Legacy of Burle
Marx.* London: Thames & Hudson, 2006.

Treib, Marc. *Thomas Church, Landscape Architect.* San
Francisco: William Stout, Publisher, 2003.

Turner, Tom. *Garden History (Philosophy and Design 2000
B.C.–2000 A.D.).* London: Spon Press, 2005.